MW00896852

Sushi Wars
Volume 1: A New Roll

A Parody by

Keith Chapman

Original Concept and Illustration by

David Wickland

Visit us at www.sushiwars.net

T-shirts, stickers and more available for your favorite Sushi Wars characters!

Copyright © 2015 Keith Chapman

All rights reserved.

ISBN-13: 978-1508882428
ISBN-10: 1508882428

DEDICATION

To my awesome boys, Derek and Tyler and
to David's awesome daughter Sophia!

May the Rice be with you!

ACKNOWLEDGMENTS

I have started many, many books on a variety of topics. This is the first one that I have actually completed. I owe thanks for that to my creative partnership with David Wickland. David is the originator of the Sushi Wars concept and core characters. He had a dream of starting a t-shirt company and Sushi Wars was the first topic. Sushi Wars is a mashup of his two loves, Star Wars and sushi, a seemingly odd pairing at first, but spend some time in that world and you might really enjoy it. With countless creative sketchbook adventures and a successful Kickstarter campaign, he created an online web store, found at sushiwars.net, where you can buy his designed Sushi Wars t-shirts and other related items including this very book. I thank David's wife, Kim, who helps with the store, ideas and product design and their daughter, Sophia, too for keeping me inspired to write. When I first saw David's prototype shirt, I immediately thought, "You need the story." I had no idea what I was actually signing up for when I made that comment but two years later, I finished Sushi Wars: A New Roll, a parody novel. We had so many long nights discussing over Guinnesses... uh, Guinni?... and online messaging over that whole time where we would discuss characters, puns, jokes, and how to convert things to sushi... normal book writing stuff, right? Roll by roll, we sushified the Star Wars universe. We had a blast doing it and the collaboration was nothing short of awesome. So, thanks, David. This has been an awesome project.

I must also acknowledge and graciously thank my wife, Becky, for her support and encouragement. Writing a novel, even a parody, especially a parody, is a labor of love and she displayed her patience and love throughout this process tolerating me staying up late at night to write. Truly, I love you!

My kids, Derek and Tyler, were the biggest part of the inspiration to write this parody novel. They enjoyed it when I would read the latest chapter just hot off the keyboard. That kept me inspired. To see your children enjoy something you write is an exceedingly addicting motivator! This one is for you guys. I love you more than you will ever know!

I want to also acknowledge my absolute favorite place to eat, Hiro Sushi, a small, very high-quality sushi bar in Scottsdale, Arizona. How they create such amazingly wonderful sushi in the desert is beyond me. I always bring business partners from Japan to Hiro Sushi with extreme confidence. I have never been let down. Each guest I have brought there simply loved it. One gentleman even said, "It's almost as good as home. Maybe same. Very, very good, Keith-san!" Hiro-san is a wonderful sushi chef and a master of his craft. Masa-san, one of the sushi chefs at Hiro, has always been kind to us and playfully interacts with our kids as he prepares amazing dishes rather effortlessly. It would be easy to assume some of the characters in Sushi Wars are based on the people at Hiro Sushi, but they are not. Hiroshi-san and Junichi-san are fictitious characters out of my own twisted brain but Hiro Sushi is where I always envisioned my story when I needed to think something through. The restaurant itself was a huge inspiration and my sons will only sit at the end of the bar because Billy, the main character of the book, always sat at the end of the bar... and because they like watching Masa-san. I held many writing sessions there and I hope to enjoy their sushi for a very long time. If you visit the Phoenix area, it is well worth the travel time! Tell them the crew at Sushi Wars sent you. Many thanks to Hiro, Leo – Hiro's son, Masa, Take, Kazu – Hiro's brother-in-law, E.J., and Steven for the fine food and legacy that Hiro Sushi is and will remain. A nod also to Hiro's sons Kishi and Riki. Hopefully we will meet in person some day soon. Thank you, Hiro-san for such a wonderful place to enjoy wonderful food and people.

I greatly respect Japanese culture and have enjoyed every trip I have made to Japan. I have made some amazing friends in Japan and they remain friends long after the business has waned at the hands of corporations. Nonetheless, without actually living in the culture, there is no way to perfectly understand the customs, nuances, and what may be considered a horrifying faux pas. So, I felt it important to say here that any faux pas generated in this parody are not intended to insult anyone. There are several American interpretations of sushi customs and even more about Japan in general and I'm sure many are inaccurate from a cultural standpoint. Hopefully these are tasteful... like good sushi itself!

I want to acknowledge the mighty George Lucas and the amazing people involved with the Star Wars franchise. Clearly, the inspiration is driven from the movie David and I grew up loving and still love to this day. We have created a parody out of complete respect and want to honor it. It is always a curious thing when writing a parody. You must borrow concepts from that which you parody without actually outright taking it. I believe we have done that here. We have strived to really make this an original work that hopefully is accepted as it was intended, a parody that pays homage to one of the greatest stories of all time that can stand on its own merits.

Finally, thank you for picking up this book. Whether you bought it, borrowed it, found it, received it as a gift or are "evaluating it for free," I simply hope you find it enjoyable. So, curl up with some green tea, eat some high quality sushi and read on!

May the Rice be with you.... always! It's sticky after all.

Keith

This page left intentionally blank... oh... whoops. Never mind.

1 IMPERIAL STARGAZERS

Hi. My name is Billy, Billy McKay. I'm 10 years old and I hate sushi.

Raw fish? Who wants to eat raw fish? I'll tell you who. My parents want to eat raw fish and it seems like every day. Ok, well it's once or twice a week but it seems like every day. My dad travels to Japan a lot for his job and well I think he thinks he's Japanese. He's not. My mom loves sushi. She hasn't been to Japan, but she is a total health freak and her weekly sushi is what she calls "her little fish treat". Ugh. Just about every Friday night, we end up taking the subway to Moto Sushi downtown. It's so predictable that Hiroshi-san, the owner and head sushi chef, saves a special place for us at the end of the sushi bar. Reserved. I sit at the very end so I don't bother people or so my mom tells me. I lean up against a bamboo wall and stare down the bar at dead fish parts sliced and diced to order. Not only do I get bored as my dad and mom socialize with the regulars and Hiroshi-san himself as he slices and wraps, but I get hungry. Hiroshi-san has attempted many times in the past to get me to try some of these things but I just keep ordering kushikatsu - fried foods on a stick. Hiroshi-san sucks his teeth every time I order kushi and asks me if I am sure I didn't say sushi. Well, I didn't and I won't.

So, now it's Friday night. Guess where I am. I swear I will be wearing through the bamboo wall with my head someday. I had a rough week at school. I failed a math test that I actually did try to study for and mom and dad didn't take kindly to that. In fact, video games were banned for an entire week until I can "figure out how to study more effectively". And this stinks because I am so close to finishing the Planet Hoth level in the latest Star Wars game. With a week off, I just know I am going to forget how I got this far in the level and I'll have to start all over again. I breezed through the New Hope levels almost as if I programmed it

1

myself. The Empire Strikes Back levels though are kicking my butt. You know, I should just bring my Star Wars action figure collection here to Moto Sushi and attack these fish like the evil Imperial forces they are. But, it would completely bum me out if I lost or broke one of my action figures battling fish. In fact, they might even start smelling like fish. That'd be worse than Luke in the trash compactor. Still, it would be cool to have an epic galactic battle in here.

"Billy-san, sushi tonight, alright," Hiroshi-san interrupted my thoughts with a forced grin.

"Kushi, Hiroshi-san," I replied, eyes about to roll.

There was a reply involving sucking of teeth and a slight sideways nod of the head to the left.

"With a 'k', ok? Kushi," I said.

"Sushi better, Billy-san." He paused. Looked at me with a new hope in his eye.

He quickly realized I was not about to budge. He gave in and confirmed, "Kushikatsu. Hai!"

Hiroshi-san then sighed and continued to suck his teeth, shaking his head ever so slightly as if he was wondering what was wrong with me.

Sushi. Raw fish. The last time my parents put sushi on my plate, it just sat there and then I got in trouble for not eating it. I just pushed it along my plate with my chopsticks. Then I decided to pretend to fight it using one of the chopsticks as a lightsaber. Then I got in trouble for that. But... what if these fish just fought themselves? Hmmm... maybe I don't need to bring my Star Wars action figures after all... I... might just have... everything... I... need... right here!

A long time to go in a Sushi Bar right, right here...
Sushi Wars: Episode IV - A New Roll
It is a period of parasitic war. Rebel spacefish, striking from a hidden plate, have won their first victory against the evil Tempura. During the battle, Rebel spies managed to steal secret plans to the Tempura's ultimate weapon, the Death Starfish, an armored starfish battle station with enough power to destroy an entire stack of plates. Pursued by the Tempura's sinister agents, Princess Maki races home aboard her spacefish, custodian of the stolen plans that can save her sushi and restore freedom to the oceanverse.

Hiroshi-san greeted my parents with a wide smile and a graciously deep bow. They engaged in some small talk about their week and how business was at the sushi bar. Then, Hiroshi-san abruptly raised his index finger in the air as if he remembered something important, reached beneath his apron, and pulled out his smartphone. He then scrolled around on the phone, raising his other hand as if to ask for patience, and then explained that his nephew in Japan had just gone deep sea diving near Mikomoto Pearl Island and filmed a video of a school of hammerhead sharks. My father was incredibly interested and watched intently as the video played on Hiroshi-san's smartphone. I peered over and Hiroshi-san shuffled closer to show me when suddenly behind him, Junichi-san, a somewhat clumsy assistant chef to Hiroshi-san, slipped behind the bar and dropped a large dead, brown fish with eyes on top of its head. Hiroshi-san looked to the ceiling and groaned his disapproval without looking as the heavily bowing Junichi-san scrambled to pick up the fish. As he raised the fish off the floor, it slipped out of his arms again and flew in my direction, hitting the bamboo wall with fish slime smattering about. Hiroshi-san swung around to face Junichi-san as his anger emerged from beneath his breath. "Rewash! Rewash! That is a back-banded stargazer! A special fish! Prepare properly and concentrate! Now!" Somehow, Hiroshi-san kept a forced smile on his face as he scolded Junichi-san in his attempt to minimize the scene. He shook his head, looked at me somewhat embarrassed, apologized for Junichi-san, and went to get another customer's order. I never really saw much of the hammerhead video.

A Rebel Hammerhead Runner firing laserbeans from the back of the spacefish emerges from behind the plate. Its pursuer, an Imperial Stargazer, fires hundreds of laserbean torpedoes in their direction. The main dorsal fin of the Rebel Hammerhead Runner disintegrates, sending shards of cartilage, slime and shark skin into the open galaxsea. The explosion rocks the Rebel spacefish.

Junichi-san quickly wiped the wall with a dish towel, looking nervously over his shoulder at Hiroshi-san. He grabbed the bruised and felled fish from the backside of the sushi bar and stuffed it into his apron, looking back and forth nervously with a grimace, severely embarrassed about the incident, ensuring he did not drop it yet again. He scuffled into the back of the restaurant like a nervous school girl, Japanese noren curtains fluttering about in his wake.

Minutes later, Junichi-san reappeared from behind the noren curtains with a nervous smile, precariously balancing 3 bowls of miso soup. I never liked soup and I certainly never liked miso soup with the floating seaweed and gelatinous cubes of white tofu. And it burned me the one time I tried it, so that was that. Junichi-san nervously laughed as he placed the miso soup in front of my parents, bowing for their approval and forgiveness. They hardly noticed but did eventually nod. As he placed the remaining bowl of miso soup by the gold-labelled soy sauce bottle in front of me, his smile eroded. He knew he would be carrying a full bowl of miso soup back into the kitchen before the next course was to be served. As he turned away, I heard him mutter, "I know best than to waste miso on boy." I know he intended me to hear it since he highly preferred speaking Japanese. His english was poor. I smiled sarcastically in case he looked back. He didn't. He just shrugged his shoulders as he shuffled away. On the wall behind him was a blackboard highlighting a special on hata, sushi made from grouper fish. Hiroshi-san placed a small bowl of edamame in front of my mom as an appetizer, placed a small plate in front of each of us, and gave me a glass of water with a bendy straw. The edamame, when squeezed, made soy beans emerge from their pods and served as great projectiles if properly cooked, or ... uh, so I have heard.

Hiroshi-san asked my parents, "Would you care for hata tonight? Good grouper on special."

My father looked up, shrugged and shook his head back and forth as he continued to look at the sushi menu.

Onboard the Rebel Hammerhead Runner, two roebots, Miso-D2 and Soy-3PO, struggle to make their way through a battered hallway as the spacefish starts to break apart. Soy-3PO, a tall, golden, waddling soyd in a soy sauce bottle form, learns they have shut down the main gastroreactor and becomes concerned for their safety. Miso-D2, a rolling miso dish with a lid, gurgles and bloops at Soy-3PO, urging him down the hallway. Rebel groupers rush past the roebots and take up battle positions in the main passageway. Their laserbeans aim at the large entry before them.

The Imperial Stargazer, a venomous, electric spacefish, immobilizes and takes over the baby Rebel Hammerhead Runner. It draws the small Rebel spacefish into it's wide frowning mouth.

Soy-3PO looks down at Miso-D2. "We're doomed! The princess will not roll away this time!"

Junichi-san emerged from the kitchen with a bowl of ikura, salmon roe, and delivered it to a customer at the other end of the sushi bar. My mother watched him speed by as she popped some edamame into her mouth. Upon his return, he dropped off a bottle of sake and 2 cups in front of my mother, uttering, "Sake for Tom-san and Linda-san. Hai."

Miso-D2 percolates and hisses as the large cartilage chunk before them is forced open by a large ikura blast. The Rebel groupers start firing their laserbeans towards the steam near the cartilage chunk. A flood of Imperial saketroopers enter the opening, firing their laserbeans. The saketroopers are armored sake bottles ready for battle at any time. The Rebel groupers flip about and cower as the laserbean blasts ricochet around them. The saketroopers are simply too strong and the Rebel groupers are driven down and back, some gutted, some filleted, and some end up belly up.

Soy-3PO wobbles down the hallway in a panic and yells out, "I should have known better than to trust the logic of a half-sized thermocapsulary tofu-stock vessel." Miso-D2 angrily replies with aggressive gurgles and shoots a small stream of steam toward Soy-3PO's direction.

I paddled the tofu around in the seaweed infested soup with the odd shaped miso spoon they always provide. I usually use the seaweed as an obstacle course for the tofu to navigate around to pass the time. No different this time. I got a bit immersed in this since there is no way I will ever eat it and was getting bored already. I was interrupted by my father making various grunts and "ahems" aimed in my direction. I stopped driving tofu and put the spoon down without looking up. I have heard those grunts and "ahems" before and they usually mean "don't play with your food" or something very similar to that, usually with increasing severity. I glanced over at my mom slurping her miso down. She caught my eye with a wink. I smirked and resumed staring into the bowl. Out of the corner of my eye, I saw Junichi-san bring over the first two dishes, one on a thin wooden plank, the other in a small white dish. The first was an order of California rolls, a type of maki, maki-zushi to be exact. The other was an order of ika, blanched squid. I know way too much about sushi for hating it. If only I liked it... even a little bit... but no, it's gross. The stock in the miso soup stopped swirling and started to settle forming an even more unappetizing film on the top surface. My mom placed a piece of ika on my dish and I quickly poured some soy sauce on top of it, and not for taste, as I had no intention of ever eating it, but to simply make it black.

Miso-D2 quickly rolls down the hallway, leaving Soy-3PO waddling after him, as Rebel groupers fall about in a hailstorm of laserbeans from the saketroopers. The Dark Lord of the Surf, Squid Vader, enters the large hole in the entryway through a large plume of steam, black tentacles flowing around him, gasps of air seeping in and out past his

5

dark mantle. Saketroopers peel off as Squid Vader propels himself down the hallway toward where the two roebot soyds, Miso-D2 and Soy-3PO, just exited.

I grabbed the darkened ika off of the stark white dish in front of me with my chopsticks and made it look like it was sliding across the bar to my mom's plate, moving the sake bottle in front of mom, out of the way. I brought the soy sauce bottle closer to the miso soup, which was now getting cold and grosser by the second. Soggy seaweed. Yuck. Any seaweed. Yuck.

Soy-3PO stands in another hallway, somewhat bewildered. Miso-D2 is nowhere in sight. The gurgling screams of the doomed Rebel groupers can be heard in the distance.

I took a California roll from the thin wood plank and placed it above my coagulating miso soup. I flicked off some of the sesame seeds into the soup and the stock began to swirl. I swished the miso around with the maki, still firmly held by my chopsticks.

"What are you doing?!" exclaimed my mom.

"Do not play with your food! That roll costs us at least a dollar! It is not to be dunked into miso like a donut. Now please just eat it, sweetie."

My mom turned to my dad and threw out a fake laugh to a joke she didn't hear which was her duty during any social time. My father was talking with a neighboring customer, telling his usual repertoire of ice-breaker jokes.

"Miso-D2! Miso-D2, where are you?" calls out Soy-3PO as he begins to wander the hallways in a near panic. Vague gurgles and bloops in the distance grab Soy-3PO's attention and he spots Miso-D2 at the end of the hallway in a steam-filled alcove. A beautiful sushi roll, Princess Maki, stands in front of Miso-D2 and puts sesame dataseeds into Miso-D2's bowl. Princess Maki, looks about, very concerned. She adjusts Miso-D2's bowl and sends him out to rejoin Soy-3PO.

Soy-3PO raises his cap and shouts, "At last! Where have you been? They're heading in this direction. What are we going to do? We'll be sent to the rice fields of Hokkaido or smashed into sea glass and clay shards or who knows what!"

Saketroopers are heard approaching. Miso-D2 rolls past his companion and races down a connecting corridor. Soy-3PO waddles after him, his soy sauce swishing about beneath his gold cap.

"Wait a minute, where are you going, you spoutless teapot?" asks Soy-3PO.

He is answered with fading gurgles and burps.

I buried the maki roll under a few tofu chunks in the now cooled miso soup and covered it further with a ridiculously large piece of seaweed. Junichi-san, seeing my parents had finished their miso, came to clear their bowls. He bowed as he offered to take them away. He stacked them in one hand and grabbed my fully loaded bowl, without offering, on his way though the noren curtains. One miso soup and one maki roll cleared the deck safely; that is, safely away from my mouth. I grabbed the rather evil looking piece of ika from my dish. Mom glanced at me and smiled. I honestly think they think I actually eat this stuff, and I think they think I actually enjoy it. Not so much!

The evil Squid Vader floats over the eviscerated and belly-up Rebel groupers and grabs a wounded Rebel grouper officer with his strongest tentacle. He stares into the Rebel's roe eye, looking for information. An Imperial seigo officer rushes up to Squid Vader and informs him that the Death Starfish plan dataseeds are not in the main brain of the Rebel Hammerhead spacefish as they had hoped. Squid Vader squeezes the Rebel grouper officer tightly with his enwrapped tentacle.

"Where are those tidemissions you intercepted?" Squid Vader asks. The Rebel officer gurgles, sea foam exiting his mouth, and explains, "We intercepted no tidemissions. This is a conuslar ship. We're on a diplomatic gastropoda mission."

"If this is a conuslar ship, where is the clambassador?" Squid Vader challenges.

The Rebel grouper officer gurgles under a tightened Squid Vader grip. The officer goes limp as an audible squish of the fish leaves his sushiform.

Squid Vader tosses the grouper officer against the wall, making another loud and wet squishing sound, and turns to his Imperial officer and says, "Clammander, tear this spacefish apart until you have found those plans and bring me the clambassador. I want her alive and uncooked!"

Saketroopers immediately scurry about the hallways, laserbean weapons drawn.

Meanwhile, Princess Maki huddles in a small alcove off the main hallway as saketroopers search the spacefish. The fear in her eyes gives way to anger as the saketroopers get closer to her. One of the saketroopers spots her and hiccups.

"There she is! Set for sear!"

Princess Maki rolls out of her hiding place and blasts a saketrooper with her laserbean pistol. She starts to escape but is felled by a paralyzing bean hitting her between the rolls. A few pieces of rice slowly dribble out of her. The saketroopers inspect her limp roll.

"She'll be alright. Inform Squid Vader that we have a prisoner, not eligible for pa-roll." Two junior saketroopers giggle under their caps.

Through the noren curtain, I saw Junichi-san cleaning out the miso soup bowls. He rinsed out the two empty bowls with the kitchen's water sprayer. He started to dump my full miso bowl into the sink, shaking his head. The maki I hid inside sat there in the open at the bottom of the miso bowl. He looked down at it, somewhat stunned, and looked back at me through the curtains with a troublesome look. He seemed like he was going to tell my parents. I just knew this was bound to happen as he came toward me with the miso bowl containing the now damp and damaged maki roll. He looked at me with a snarling nod, made sure my parents weren't looking, and dumped the miso bowl's contents onto the plate in front of me. There sat the soggy maki roll in the center of the plate next to the blackened ika, a few sesame seeds falling onto my plate. He smiled at me, winked evilly, and returned to the kitchen with the near empty, sesame-seed-infested miso bowl and placed it and other dishes into a small dishwasher.

Junichi-san closed the small glass door on the dishwasher and pushed a button on the front panel. A red light started flashing and the dishwasher began jiggling back and forth as jet streams of soapy water hit the miso bowls. Bottles of soy sauce on top of the small dishwasher started rattling and vibrating as the dishwasher went about its mission.

Miso-D2 stops at the end of a hallway before a small hatch of an emergency escape egg. He snaps the embryonic seal on the main hatch and a red warning pulse on the germinal disc begins to flash. Miso-D2 enters the cramped fish egg.

Soy-3PO chases after Miso-D2 and warns him, "Hey, you are not permitted in there. It's restricted... and restricting! You'll be shelved for sure or reborn as a baby hammerhead!"

Miso-D2 burps at him.

"Don't call me a capless philosopher with the glass half empty, you overweight bowl of tofu! Now come out before someone orders more miso!"

Miso-D2 whistles and burps at his reluctant companion.

"Secret mission? What plans? What are you talking about? I'm not getting in there! It's gooey."

Miso-D2 aggressively gurgles at Soy-3PO and quivers from side to side, hot liquid spilling out either side of his bowl.

An explosion emanates from the main hallway sending cartilage flying near Soy-3PO. Miso-D2 hisses and burps furiously at Soy-3PO.

Soy-3PO drops and rolls into the spacefish's escape egg and exclaims, "I'm going to regret you egging me on like this. I'm likely to crack!"

In the control room, on the main viewer membrane of the Imperial Stargazer, Imperial seigo pilots watch another escape egg speed away from the heavily damaged Rebel Hammerhead Runner. The captain holds his cap up high as a signal to wait.

"Hold your fire. There are no sushiforms. It must be unfertilized and ejected by the damaged nervous system."

Inside the escape egg, Miso-D2 and Soy-3PO observe the damaged Rebel Hammerhead Runner and the Imperial Stargazer as they drift away. Soy-3PO initiates a detailed inquiry about the safety and goopiness of the escape egg with Miso-D2. Miso-D2 hisses and gurgles assuringly and resumes observing the damaged spacefish.

I took the ika up once again with my chopsticks and marched it over close to the soggy maki roll in the center of my plate. Junichi-san, sensing something awry, turned quickly from the dishwasher and thrust his head out through the curtain's opening. He gave me the stink-eye as he watched me march the ika to the maki roll, his brow furrowed. I figured he was getting upset with me playing with my food, so I thought maybe I should taunt him a little. I noticed that mom and dad were preoccupied with their socializing as usual, so I smacked the maki on the plate with my tightly held chunk of squid. I moved the sake bottle in front of my mom closer to my plate when she wasn't looking. This was risky. I'm not supposed to touch the sake bottles.

Princess Maki is led down a smaller hallway by a squad of laserbean-blaster-equipped saketroopers, her nori bound by a soba noodle. She has trouble keeping up with the fast wobbling saketroopers and they brutally shove her forward in order to keep her in pace. They stop in a steamy hallway as Squid Vader emerges from the shadows. The sinister Dark Lord of the Surf stares hard at the frail, young seanator, but she doesn't roll an inch.

Princess Maki's anger rises as she speaks. "Squid Vader. I should have known. Only you could be so bold… and covered in such black inky, soy sauce. The Imperial Seanate will not float for this. When they

9

hear you've attacked a conuslar..."

Squid Vader interrupts in a harsh tone, "Don't play shell games with me, Your Gai-ness. You weren't on any mercy roll missions this time. You passed directly through a restricted intertidal zone. Several tidemissions were beaned to this spacefish by Rebel spies. I want to know what happened to the plans they sent you."

"I don't know what you're talking about. I'm a member of the Imperial Seanate on a conuslar mission to Abaloneraan..."

Squid Vader raises a rather large and ominous tentacle. "You are part of the Rebel Alliance... and a traitor! Roll her away!"

My parents were laughing at a joke they likely didn't get so I dropped the ika on my dish and fully grabbed the nearby sake bottle. I smacked the maki roll with the side of the bottle. Now, I knew I could get in trouble for even moving the bottle of sake, but I risked it. I'm only 10 years old and you have to be 21 or something to drink from these bottles, but I was actually having fun for once and I wasn't about to just sit there staring at the back wall, banging my head against the bamboo. So, the sake continued to be in play!

Princess Maki is marched away down the hallway into the steaming entrance created by the saketroopers' initial ikura blast. An Imperial Clammander turns to Squid Vader and nervously suggests that holding Princess Maki is dangerous as it may spawn sympathy for the Rebellion in the seanate if word gets out. Squid Vader dismisses the Clammander's concerns as he views Princess Maki as the only link he has to the Rebel's secret plate.

The Imperial Clammander warns, "She'll spoil before she tells you anything."

Squid Vader replies, "Leave that to me. Send a distress signal and then inform the seanate that all aboard were boiled or fried!"

I smacked the maki again with the sake bottle but accidentally hit my plate which made a rather obnoxious clink noise. Mom immediately turned her head in my direction and saw my hand on the sake bottle. "Billy!" she exclaimed. "You, mister, are not allowed to drink that! That is alcohol and alcohol is bad for a young boy like yourself! Now, take your hand off that bottle and eat your squid and roll. My Lord!" Dad snarled in my direction and then resumed his smile to the neighboring customer shaking his head and resumed chatting endlessly about Japanese eating customs that he knew very little about.

A second Imperial seigo officer approaches the Dark Lord and the Clammander and abruptly snaps to attention waiting for acknowledgement to speak. He informs his leaders that the battle station plans are not aboard the Rebel Hammerhead Runner spacefish and that no tidemissions were made. He informs them that an escape egg was jettisoned during the fight, but no sushiforms were on board.

"She must have hidden the plans in the escape egg. Send a case of saketroopers down to retrieve them. See to it personally, Clammander. There'll be no one to stop us this time," orders Squid Vader.

"Yes, sir! I will send a sake party underway immediately!" barks the Clammander.

I looked at Mom ready with an explanation but immediately got trumped by her punishing mom-look. "Yes, ma'am," I said in a dropping tone. The first course was thankfully done, but more sushi was most certainly on the way.

2 TIDETOOINE

Junichi-san came over to clear the remaining dishes and boards from the first course, paving the way for the next sushi wave. I was still awaiting my kushi. Fried foods have historically taken remarkably longer than raw fish here. I thought it was just a way of trying to get me to consider eating sushi but that won't happen. I can be patient when I want to be.

Junichi-san tried to get my dad's attention by gently calling to him, "McKay-san. Uh... Mistel Tom." He knew little of our social customs in America and he was trying to improve his english but was having a difficult time. My dad said he often confused the letters "R" and "L" apparently because the Japanese language has a single consonant sound in place for both of these letter sounds. He also said not to forget that Junich-san's English is way better than my Japanese so I shouldn't judge. I didn't care how he spoke and don't care to make fun of it. Dad was actually right. Imagine how bad my Japanese would be if I even tried to speak it. I was more concerned about him trying to get me to eat sushi or get me in trouble. Plus there are so many other things to make fun of when it comes to Junichi-san!

Junichi-san glanced at me quickly and addressed my dad, "Tom-san, uh... I clee-ah...ah, clear prates... sorry, clear plates... now. Ok? Ok. Uh... ika, one piece... re... le... left? Um... Birr... no... Billy-san eat?" A devious smile emerged on his face.

I knew it. He was trying to make me eat a piece of blanched squid by suggesting it to my dad. I was thinking that when he cleared the maki board, he was going to tell my dad I hid one in the miso but I think his plan was to force me to eat the squid. Nice try. Fortunately, the Force was weak with this one. My dad did not want to be interrupted from his discussion with the neighboring sushi customer. He was fully engaged.

He nodded at Junichi-san with a quick glance in his direction, not really hearing what he said. Junichi-san glared at me as the devious smile converted to an evil smile. I sarcastically smiled back at him and shrugged my shoulders. Junichi-san placed the last piece of ika on my dish and cleared the rest of the dishes. He never got the chance to rat me out on the hidden maki roll as my dad unknowingly dismissed him with his aimless nod and I was certainly not about to eat this ika on my plate either. I started watching the dishwasher through the slit in the noren curtains. It was making a lot of noise. The soy sauce bottles on top rattled about loudly.

The Imperial Stargazer glides over the surface of a nearby plate, Tidetooine, a "No Fish's Sea" of a plate where the rugged ocean waters meet the foreboding dark skies, with no land in sight. The Dark Lord of the Surf and his case of saketroopers had begun to give chase to the escape egg that was jettisoned off the Rebel Hammerhead Runner.

The two helpless soyds, Miso-D2 and Soy-3PO, kick up mists of seawater as they leave the half-sunken escape egg. They clumsily work their way across the water's surface, bobbing amongst the dark waves. Miso-D2 uses his water stream jets to propel forward while Soy-3PO aimlessly bobs, adrift.

Soy-3PO complains, "How did I get into this mess? A glass bottle adrift on an ocean plate. I really don't know how. We seem to be made to suffer. It's our roll in life."

Miso-D2 simply responds with encouraging gurgling and bubbling tones as Soy-3PO begins to roll forward slowly using his cap to paddle, following Miso-D2.

Soy-3PO continues, "I've got to rest before I fill up with water! And my cap is almost rusted! What an unforgiving plate this is."

Suddenly, Miso-D2 changes direction and starts off in the direction of the choppiest water with high crashing waves. Soy-3PO stops paddling with his cap and yells at him. "Where are you going?" he asks. Miso-D2 responds with informative hisses.

"Well, I am not going that way. It's much too choppy. This way is much easier."

Miso-D2 counters with a long whistle.

"What makes you think there are land settlements over there?"

Miso-D2 makes more burping sounds.

"Don't get soupy with me you cracked pot."

Miso-D2 continues burping and whistling.

"What mission? What are you talking about? I've had just about enough of you! Go that way! You'll be soupless within a day, you seasick, steamed vessel!"

Soy-3PO splashes toward Miso-D2 and starts paddling off in the direction of the calmer open sea.

"And don't let me catch you following me, begging for help, because you won't get it, you poor excuse for a bobber."

Miso-D2 replies with rude burps and starts streaming towards the rough seas ahead.

"No more careless adventures. I'm not going that way!"

The two soyds part ways.

Junichi-san returned to the kitchen through the curtains and placed the dishes in the sink. He then removed the soy sauce bottles on top of the rickety dishwasher and placed them on a tray. The loud rattling stopped.

Soy-3PO, wet and tired, struggles across the vast sea surface and turns to look in the direction from which he came. He could no longer spot Miso-D2 or the choppy waves he left behind.

Soy-3PO starts talking to himself. "That cracking little bowl. This is all his fault! He tricked me into going this way, but he'll do no better. I bet they find him adrift in the middle of a soyl spill!"

Frustrated, Soy-3PO sits adrift in a vast sea of emptiness and tries to scratch off the oxidation on his cap along his glass body. His situation seems hopeless, when a slight reflection of light in the distance catches his attention. A large vessel is seen floating on the horizon.

"Wait, what's that? A traysport! I'm saved!"

Soy-3PO waves his cap frantically, bobbing up and down feverishly, swinging his rusting cap about, as he yells for attention at the large object moving toward him.

Hiroshi-san approached my dad asking if they were ready for the next course. My dad graciously nodded. Hiroshi-san nodded in return and placed a white dish of atsuage, broiled tofu, on the bar near mom. At least that stuff was cooked and I really didn't mind it so much. You could say it was the hero of the meal so far. Tofu is made from soy and it really isn't bad when cooked. If it floats around in my soup, I really don't like it but if cooked then it didn't seem too bad. A purple radish sat on the dish for decoration, cut-up and arranged like a star with six arms.

Back on Tidetooine, near a seaweed settlement in the cross-shadow of two lamps on the horizon, a lone tofu figure, Luke Soywalker, works on a large, battered land solidifier which sticks out above the sea's

14

surface. The land solidifier looks much like a large pipe with control valves that is used to mine the sea floor for raw dirt that can be used to make floating islands so seaweed will be accessible for the settlement. It provided housing, protection, food, and was incredibly important for life on Tldetooine for all sushiforms. A world of unending ocean was not of much use for sushiform habitats. However, creating landmass while growing and connecting a variety of seaweed as sustainable islands, sushiforms could not only survive but influence the entire world of Tidetooine, maybe the galaxsea, and perhaps even the oceanverse. Land solidifiers gave Tidetooine sushiforms a fighting chance on such a desperate plate.

Luke turns the control valves in hopes to start a new island for his uncle. He is aided by a beat-up, radashian, paddle-roebot with six flat, near-useless fins. The little roebot appears to be barely functioning and moves with jerky motions, causing massive ripples in the water. A bright sparkle in the morning sky catches Luke's eye and he instinctively grabs a pair of electro-finoculars from his utility belt. He stands transfixed for a few moments studying the galaxsea before him, then dashes toward his dented, crudely repaired trayspeeder, a beaten traysport that travels a few inches above the ocean on a hydro-biological field. He motions for the tiny roebot to follow him. The tiny roebot starts paddling in a tight circle as Luke yells at it. Steam begins to pour out of one of the main fins and the other fins start to brown. The roebot begins taking on water and starts to sink. Luke, disgusted with the roebot, jumps in his trayspeeder and leaves the flailing roebot to submerge itself under a plume of steam.

No one seemed to notice the atsuage so I grabbed one from the serving dish with my chopsticks. Before bringing it to my plate though, I walked it around the plate stopping at each of the other tofu blocks on the plate. This, I was going to try to eat. Otherwise, I might have starved. The kushi still hadn't arrived. I dropped the atsuage onto a small soy sauce dish and transported it over to my plate. I eventually ate the rest of atsuage keeping the first one on my plate.

Luke pilots his trayspeeder to a nearby seaweed settlement and stops outside an island that houses a power station for the seaweed settlement. Luke bursts into the power station's control room and starts yelling at several of his friends, excited to tell them about his discovery with his finoculars, a battle in the sky above Tidetooine! He is surprised to be greeted by an old friend, Baigai, a hot shot water snail that left for the Aclamademy so he could leave Tidetooine and fight in the battles, something Luke thought about a lot.

While catching up with Baigai, Luke suddenly remembers his discovery and excitedly explains that he saw a battle above the skies of Tidetooine, a battle that he just knew was between the Rebellion and the Tempura. All of his friends, including Baigai, give him a hard time and pass his discovery off as just another freighter. What would the Tempura want with a wastewater of a plate like Tidetooine? Luke begrudgingly passes it off, doubting his friends' judgement the entire time. He and Baigai wander from the group and catch up more in private.

"Luke, I didn't come back to Tidetooine just to say goodbye. I shouldn't tell you this, but you're the only one I can trust... and if I don't come back, I want somebody to know."

Luke's eyes widen with expectation and confusion. "What are you talking about?"

"I made some friends at the Aclamademy. When our spacefish goes to one of the central tidal zones, we're going to jump ship and join the Alliance."

Luke, stunned and amazed, is almost speechless. "Join the Rebellion?! Are you kidding? How?"

Baigai nervously looks around, ducks into his small shell a bit, and tries to quiet down his friend. Baigai knows it is a long shot of a plan but he needs to be part of the side that resonates with him, the side he can believe in. Luke agrees but is frustrated because he cannot join the Aclamademy because he must help his uncle fend off the raiding schools of Clampeople, shellfish nomad scavenger clams trying to survive in a hostile world by plundering settlements. The Clampeople have recently been raiding the outskirts of their settlements and if he doesn't help his uncle defend their land solidifiers, his uncle's livelihood could be in danger. Luke delayed his application to the Aclamademy for one full season. He can't leave him now. He has Clampeople to shuck.

Baigai cheers up his friend with encouraging words about Luke being able to leave Tidetooine someday. Baigai plans to leave Tidetooine in the morning. They say their goodbyes, wondering if they will ever see each other again.

Junichi-san quickly short-stepped across the back of the sushi bar gathering as many dishes as he could from each patron. When he arrived in front of me, he had a stack of dishes and boards leaning on his chest, held there by his shaky left hand. The dishes rattled. He expected to not need to grab any dishes in front of me but upon seeing that I nearly finished the atsuage, he jerked back in surprise. The dishes started toppling but with quick reflexes, Junichi-san kept them all from falling. His brow broke into a sweat as he looked over his crouched shoulder with a wince on his face, expecting an abrupt scolding from Hiroshi-san.

Fortunately for Junichi-san, Hiroshi-san was furiously preparing a sushi dish and simultaneously engaged in conversation with a patron at the other side of the sushi bar and seemed not to notice or care. Junichi-san re-balanced all the dishes, smiled nervously at me, and grabbed the empty atsuage serving dish from the bar in front of me. I winked at him as if to say his secret of nearly breaking a stack of dishes was safe with me but also to imply that I might reserve the right to use information like this to get what I want from him, when I want. He responded with a grimace and shuffled through the curtains into the kitchen, dishes clinking merrily.

Hiroshi-san made his way over to my father, nodding with another dish in hand. He placed a small dish containing three cuts of engawa, a flute fish fillet with green roe decoration. It was a nice presentation... for sushi. I raised my hand as the dish landed in front of mom. Hiroshi-san bowed at me, eyes meeting mine with a questioning look.

"Kushi done yet?" I asked.

Hiroshi-san sucked his teeth and glanced into the kitchen. He clapped for Junichi-san.

"Kushikatsu for Billy-san?"

Junichi-san shrugged his shoulders and went back into the kitchen to check on my kushikatsu. I may never eat tonight. The atsuage just made me hungrier. Hiroshi-san waved at me and pointed to the kitchen suggesting that Junichi-san was on it. Great.

My mom put an engawa fillet on my plate, smiled at me, and nodded as she lifted her head. Yeah... I'm not eating this. But... I will play with this.

Miso-D2 drifts amid some rather choppy waves with a foreboding mist emerging from the surface of the darkening Tidetooine ocean. Miso-D2 pulses his underwater jet streams and cautiously fineuvers through the ominous crests of waves. He inadvertently makes a loud clicking noise as he switches from a pulsing jet stream to a constant flow. He hears a distant, hissing sound and stops his streams for a moment. He sits adrift listening. Convinced he is alone, he continues on his way. In the distance, a splash of seawater rises over a wave crest and a small figure darts behind the next wave. A little further beyond the crest, a slight flicker of light reveals a pair of green roe-eyes in the dark water only a small distance from Miso-D2.

The unsuspecting Miso-D2 streams along until suddenly, beyond the nearest crest, a powerful green algal ray shoots out from the wave and engulfs Miso-D2 in an eerie, slimy glow. The algae covering him oozes into his inner bowl and his steam jets uncontrollably blast fully on, then off, then on, then off again with no sign of movement. From beneath the waves emerge three Engawas, no larger than Miso-D2 himself. They holster strange and complex algal weapons as they cautiously approach the inactive Miso-D2. They are small, feathered fish tails encloaked in a dark seaweed with only their glowing green roe-eyes visible. They hiss to one another and wrap the heavy Miso-D2 in seaweed that they tie to their nori. They tug him off through the wave crests, his bowl barely afloat in the rough seas.

As I played with the raw fish in front of me... what else is there to do with it... Dad ordered more sake. Whenever they order more sake it means we will likely be closing the restaurant down. Dad has said several times this week that his work has been very challenging and that he needs to relax. His drinking of sake tends to relax him and his drinking of sake tends to provoke Mom. Might as well settle in. It could be a long night.

They must have been flying the kushikatsu in direct from Japan. Still no sign of what I ordered about 20 minutes ago. I think this is Junichi-san's plan. He thinks if the kid is hungry enough, he'll eat sushi. I was hungry, hungry enough to wait for what I ordered and foil his evil plan.

Behind the noren curtains, I saw Junichi-san taking some serving trays out of the dishwasher. He started stacking them on a drying rack. They were set to drip dry over the already soaked counter.

The Engawas tug Miso-D2 out of the rough seas, beyond the crests of the large waves, to an impressively large floating traysport vessel constructed by stacked trays connected by a matrix of large beans and pea pods. They wrap Miso-D2 in a towelette, covering his bowl, and then put him under a large straw hanging down on the side of the traysport. The roebot is sucked into the straw and onto the giant traysport. The Engawas swish around the base of the vessel, inch up narrow chopstick ladders and enter the main tray of the behemoth traysport.

Junichi-san unloaded more dishes from the dishwasher and stacked the miso bowls on top of the drying serving trays.

It is dim inside the holding area of the Engawa Traysport. Miso-D2 finds himself amidst a scrap heap of other roebots, grotesquely twisted and maimed. Glass, plastic, wood, clay and metal pieces lie about everywhere. Miso-D2 squirms out of the towelette enough to switch on a small floodlight on his bowl and stumbles around the scrap heap. As he bumps into various parts, he lets out a pathetic whimper and makes his way to what appears to be an opening at the end of the eerie chamber. He enters a room with a very low ceiling and sees a dozen or so roebots engaged in conversation. Suddenly, a familiar voice emerges from the noisy gurgles and clicks.

"Miso-D2! It's you! It's you!" cries a battered and tattered Soy-3PO as he attempts to place his cap around his lost companion.

The large Engawa Traysport motors off toward the setting twin lamps of Tidetooine.

Hiroshi-san brought another bottle of sake over to my parents and poured each of them a small serving of the clear liquid in their ochokos, the small sake cups. He smiled and offered his hands forward, raised them with an encouraging motion and bowed as he dismissed himself to tend to other customers. They drank.

Imperial saketroopers bob about in open water, inspecting the half-submerged escape egg that brought Miso-D2 and Soy-3PO to Tidetooine. A saketrooper finds a small stain of soy sauce on the fish escape egg. He yells across the waves to an officer some distance away and informs him that they have found evidence of soyds. They conclude that the egg must have contained soyds or roebots that escaped from the Rebel Hammerhead Runner. They spot a trail of small soyl spills on the surface of the vast ocean leading them towards the setting lamps of Tidetooine.

Meanwhile, the Engawa Traysport continues to motor across rough seas and finally docks at a remote seaweed settlement near a floating island. Miso-D2 and Soy-3PO noisily bounce about in the holding room. Miso-D2 appears to be cold. Soy-3PO tries to wake Miso-D2. Suddenly, the shaking and bouncing of the traysport stops, creating quite a commotion amongst all of the roebots in the holding room. Soy-3PO bangs the bowl of Miso-D2. Miso-D2 steams up and gurgles. At the far end of the chamber, a hatch opens filling the tray with a blinding light. A dozen or so Engawas enter looking over the es-cargo.

Soy-3PO utters, "This is fishy. We're doomed."

An Engawa moves toward them.

"Do you think they will melt us down?" asks Soy-3PO.

Miso-D2 responds with an unassuring burp.

"Don't shoot! Don't shoot! Will this never end? My soy is coagulating."

Junichi-san, still working in the kitchen, removed the dry dishes from the drying rack and placed them on the shelf. He arranged them very specifically such that the Japanese characters on the sides of the miso bowls lined up just perfectly. As he did this, he looked out through the curtains to see if Hiroshi-san was nearby. Apparently, the sloppy alignment of bowls has been an issue in the past. He then looked over the bottles of soy sauce stacked on the shelf behind the sushi bar and rotated each bottle so the gold labels all lined up. He then quickly dusted each bottle off with his dish towel.

The Engawas utter gibberish as they go about their work to line up their battered, captive soyds and roebots. They finipulate the soyds and roebots, including Soy-3PO and Miso-D2, onto their own floating seaweed pods in front of the enormous Engawa Traysport. Near the seaweed settlement is a sushi-made island consisting of three large wooden trays recessed into the island surrounded by several tall land solidifiers and one small refrigerated home, the chilly abode of Luke's aunt and uncle. Without decent soyds and roebots to maintain this settlement, there would be no refrigeration or solid land for sushiforms and kushiforms in this area crucial to their survival on Tidetooine. They would otherwise become food for the many live and vicious fish under the surface of the Tidetooine ocean and likely be devoured within minutes.
The Engawas scurry around fussing over the roebots, straightening them up, brushing some dust from the bottles, or scrubbing down the bowls with a towelette. The nori shrouded little fish tails, known as the Engawa, smell horribly, attracting many small sea insects to their immediate area.

Hiroshi-san busily pushed past Junichi-san to enter the kitchen. A few minutes later, he emerged with my kushikatsu! It was about time. I was starving. In front of me, he unceremoniously placed a dish containing one ton katsu, a fried pork cutlet, and one bifu katsu, a fried beef cutlet, each arranged on a stick. Finally, I was able to eat something not made of tofu. I heard Hiroshi-san suck his teeth as he gently shook his head side to side and moved on to tend to another customer.

Out of the shadows of a slime-covered side building made from seaweed, limps O-Ton Katsu, a large, aging, crispy pork kushiform. He is responsible for the upkeep of this island settlement. Sushiforms and kushiforms alike depend on the work and guidance of these land farmers in order to survive the barren oceanic terrain. O-Ton takes his job very seriously. His brown, saucy eyes get lost amongst his crispy, dual-lamp-tattered skin as he squints to look over the various soyds and roebots before him. His seemingly bored nephew, Luke Soywalker, follows closely. One of the Engawas lead them through each roebot and gives an unintelligible sales pitch in a rather odd language. A voice calls out from one of the recessed wooden trays that form the island's homestead. Luke goes over to the edge of the tray and sees his Aunt Bifu, another crispy kushiform only of beef, standing in the main courtyard. His Aunt Bifu reminds Luke to make sure his Uncle O-Ton gets a translator that speaks Buri. Luke is doubtful of their success due to the poor selection of soyds. Buri is an interplatetary language created by old merchant yellowtails in part to communicate between spacefish pilots, crayfish, and support personnel when native languages were unknown and ineffective. There are slim pickings amongst the available soyds so he remains doubtful.

O-Ton reviews each soyd and comes across Soy-3PO. The lead Engawa excitedly pushes the sale of Soy-3PO onto O-Ton.

"I have no need for a protocol soyd," O-Ton states bluntly, raising his cutlet.

Soy-3PO quickly responds, "Sir, not in an environment such as this. That's why I've been programmed for over thirty secondary functions that…"

"What I really need is a soyd that understands the binary language of land solidifiers."

"Solidifiers! Sir, my first job was programming binary load lifters… very similar to your solidifiers. You could say…" O-Ton interrupts, "Do you speak Buri?

"Of course I can, sir. It's like a second language for me… I'm as fluent in Buri…"

"All right! Shut up!"

"Shutting up, sir."

O-Ton confirms the purchase of Soy-3PO to the Engawa leader. He points to another small red ochoko soyd and continues to negotiate.

I raised my hand as I looked over to Junichi-san behind the bar and tried to get his attention. He was still arranging bottles of soy sauce and other condiments. I cleared my throat loudly. Mom glared at me to be more polite. But it worked anyway. Junichi-san hesitantly turned around and nodded to me as he leaned toward me, cautiously.

"Junichi-san, may I please get some katsu sauce?"

"Katsu sauce. Hai!"

He reached up to the top shelf to get a very small, shallow dish and a bottle of katsu sauce. He popped open the cap and dabbed a tiny bit of sauce onto the small coaster-sized dish. He handed it me with a smirk and a bow. He placed it next to the soy sauce bottle by my plate, satisfied that I was not up to something.

"Hey, Junich-san, what are you trying to pull here?"

Junichi-san shrugged, very confused. He became suspicious.

"You know I like katsu sauce. I'll need a bigger dish than this... filled with sauce, please. Fill? You know... more."

Junichi-san sighed heavily, looked down for a second at the small dish, and turned to fill a nearby miso bowl with katsu sauce.

"That's better. Thanks," I said.

In broken english, he replied, "Ah... no good taste. Much sauce, no meat. Just sauce. Saucy meat."

He sucked his teeth and continued to shake his head side to side as he shuffled away.

O-Ton instructs Luke to take the two soyds over to their garage and clean them up before dinner. Luke complains about the chore but realizes he has no choice in the matter. He calls over Soy-3PO and the little red ochoko soyd but the red soyd has trouble following orders. As the Engawas start to lead the remaining roebots back into the Traysport, Miso-D2 lets out a pathetic little burp and starts jetting after his old friend, Soy-3PO. He is restrained by a slimy Engawa, who snaps him with a wet towelette. The crack is heard across the island and stops Miso-D2 immediately, setting his top bowl slightly askew and dripping. O-Ton is still negotiating with the head Engawa. Luke and the two purchased roebots finally start off for the garage when a large plume of steam emerges from the head of the red hydro-soyd and sprays sake wildly in the air. Luke informs his uncle that this ochoko soyd is clearly defective.

O-Ton confronts the lead Engawa, "Hey, what're you trying to push on us?!"

The Engawa responds with a loud and excited explanation in an indecipherable rant. Meanwhile, Miso-D2 sneaks out of line and jumps up and down on his seaweed pod making ripples across the shore of the island in hopes of getting Luke's attention. Soy-3PO nudges Luke and informs him that this blue and white miso bowl soyd is in prime condition, a real bargain.

Luke informs his uncle, who, in turn, negotiates with the lead Engawa to exchange the red one for the blue one. The Engawa reluctantly agrees. Luke motions for Miso-D2 to come over and head to the garage as his uncle pays a complaining Engawa.

Soy-3PO leans in toward Miso-D2 and says "Now, don't you forget this! Why I should stick my cap out for you is quite beyond my capacity! I should've let them bowl you over."

As I started to dig into my kushi, I realized I hadn't yet used the cold, damp towelette they always provide in a clear wrapper. So, I opened up the wrapper and washed my hands, and then I washed the outside of the miso bowl and the outside of the soy sauce bottle, mimicking Junichi-san, secretly hoping he might catch me doing this. I've always enjoyed provoking him a little bit. Not sure why. I then grabbed a toothpick off the top of the bar and started running it along the outside of the miso bowl, scratching it up and down, without leaving a mark.

Miso-D2, Soy-3PO, and Luke Soywalker enter into the wooden tray garage at the peaceful Katsu homestead. Soy-3PO lowers himself into a large tub filled with warm soyl. Near the battered trayspeeder, little Miso-D2 rests on a large barrel of miso with a hose connected to his bowl.

Soy-3PO celebrates the moment as he comments, "Thank the Chef! This soyl bath is going to feel so good. I've got such a bad case of sea-salt contamination, I can barely move!" Miso-D2 gurgles a muffled reply.

Luke seems to be lost in thought as he runs his glob of soy over the damaged fin of a small two-sushi Duskyhopper spacefish resting in a low hangar of the garage. Finally, Luke's frustrations get the better of him and he slams a toothpick across the workbench and yells out, "It just isn't fair! Oh, Baigai is right. I'm never gonna get out of here!"

Soy-3PO offers to help somehow but Luke realizes there is nothing a soyd can do for him. So, he lightens up and familiarizes himself with the new soyds. Soy-3PO exits the soyl bath as Luke starts to work on Miso-D2 with a very small, chrome toothpick, prying small algal and salt debris from between his bowl seams.

"You got a lot of salt scoring here. It looks like you soyds have seen a lot of action," says Luke curiously.

Soy-3PO replies, "With all we've been through, sometimes I'm amazed we're in as good condition as we are, what with the Rebellion and all.We've seen a lot of the galaxsea."

"You know of the Rebellion?"

"That's how we came to be in your service, if you take my meaning, sir."

Luke becomes very interested and asks, "Have you been in many battles? Well, I mean for a bowl and a bottle..."

Soy-3PO responds, "Several, I think. Actually, there's not much to tell. I'm not much more than an interpreter, and not very good at telling stories. Well, not at making them interesting, anyways. After all, I'm full of condiment, not much in the way of an actual meal."

I ate a piece of ton kushikatsu after dunking it in the miso bowl filled with katsu sauce. It wasn't too bad tasting actually. Around the kushi still on my plate, there were garnishes of shredded cabbage and damp seaweed. Gag. Why was this on my plate?

I rolled some of the sticky seaweed around the shredded cabbage and made it all into a tight roll with my chopsticks. I put two smaller pieces of seaweed on the outside of the main roll containing the cabbage and placed it in front of the miso bowl containing the katsu sauce. The creation looked like a very lame California roll or maybe a green and white picture of one. My mom gently slapped me on the back of the head.

"Stop playing with your food, Billy!"

I stopped. For a second.

Luke struggles to remove a small fragment from Miso-D2's main bowl seam. Using a larger toothpick, he breaks the fragment loose with a snap, sending Luke tumbling to the garage floor. A sesame data seed, once lodged in the bowl seam, automatically slides into a slot in Miso-D2's bowl. A three-dimensional rollogram of Princess Maki Organa, the Rebel seanator, appears in front of Miso-D2 emanating from a roe lens in the main bowl. The image is a rainbow of colors as it flickers and jiggles in the dimly lit garage. Luke's mouth hangs open in awe.

"Help me, Obi-Wan Wasabi. You're my only hope," says Princess Maki in the rollogram.

Luke is incredibly interested in the rollogram and is swept by the beauty of Princess Maki. He asks Miso-D2 what this rollogram is but Miso-D2 looks about and sheepishly burps an answer for Soy-3PO to translate. Princess Maki repeats the fragmented phrase over and over again. Soy-3PO tells Luke that Miso-D2 says it is nothing, just a malfunction, a stuck piece of tofu, and that he should pay it no mind.

Luke persists, "Who is she? She's beautiful."

"I'm afraid I'm not quite sure, sir," replies Soy-3PO.

"Help me, Obi-Wan Wasabi. You're my only hope," repeated Princess Maki.

Soy-3PO continues, "I think she was a passenger on our last voyage. A roll of some importance, sir, I believe. Our captain was attached to…"

Luke interrupts, "Is there more to this rollogram?"

Luke reaches out to Miso-D2 but he abruptly spins away and lets out a variety of burps and whistles. Soy-3PO scolds Miso-D2 and encourages him to trust Luke, their new master. Miso-D2 whistles and hisses more to Soy-3PO.

Soy-3PO interprets, "He says he's the property of Obi-Wan Wasabi, a resident of these parts. And it's a private message for him. Quite frankly, sir, I don't know what he's talking about. Our last master was Captain Ama-ebi, but with what we've been through, this little bowl has become a bit eccentric, perhaps a little warped."

I sculpted a small lump of wasabi paste that came with the engawa order into a round body. I wrapped that wasabi lump with a piece of seaweed left on one of the serving trays and made the lump look a bit like a hermit crab or like someone living in a very small cave.
"Billy!"
"What?! Oh, sorry, mom."
I dismantled the sculpture.

Luke thinks for a minute and asks, "Obi-Wan Wasabi? I wonder if he means old Zen Wasabi?"

"I beg your pardon, sir, but do you know what he's talking about?"

"Well, I don't know anyone named Obi-Wan, but old Zen lives out beyond the Funamori sea ruins. He's kind of a strange old hermit crab. Well, not a crab, really… but, you know what I mean. He's a bit rooted."

Luke continues to gaze at Princess Maki and wonders who she is and asks Miso-D2 to play back the whole recording. Soy-3PO informs Luke that Miso-D2 has a restraining towelette around his bowl that is preventing him from accessing and sharing more. Luke thinks Miso-D2 is too small to swim away from him anyway so he removes the restraining towelette with some meat shears.

As the restraining towelette falls away, Luke proudly and eagerly states, "There you go!" fully expecting to see the full recording now.

The Princess immediately disappears. Luke cries out to bring her back. Soy-3PO rolls up in embarrassment as Miso-D2 gurgles innocently.

"What message? The rollogram you're carrying inside your salty innards!" scolds Soy-3PO.

Luke's aunt, Bifu Katsu, calls out from another room for Luke to come to dinner. Luke calls back to state he is on his way, stands up, and shakes about in disappointment.

Soy-3PO feels obligated to apologize for Miso-D2's behavior, "I'm sorry, sir, but he appears to have picked up a slight mold and is malfunctioning."

Luke asks Soy-3PO to see what he can do with Miso-D2 and that he'll return shortly.

Soy-3PO addresses Miso-D2, "Just you reconsider playing that rollogram for him."

Miso-D2 burps in response.

"No, I don't think he likes you at all," he says. Miso-D2 burps again.

"No, I don't like you either. You're quite soyled."

I continued to eat my beef and pork kushi and actually enjoyed it for once. Junichi-san glanced over at my plate to see if I was eating. He shook his head when he saw that I had been. I have always suspected that if my parents didn't spend so much money and time here, Junichi-san would poison me or something. Instead of worrying about that, I resumed playing with my food. I walked the last piece of atsuage on my plate with my chopsticks to meet up with my kushi and dropped it on the kushi plate in front of me.

Luke returns to the homestead at his aunt's request to eat dinner. He argues with his Aunt Bifu and Uncle O-Ton about the soyds, old Zen Wasabi, and Luke's commitment to staying on for land harvesting one more season. Resigned to his fate, Luke leaves the dining area and returns to the garage to finish cleaning the soyds for their new duties. Before he enters the garage, he watches the twin lamps of Tidetooine slowly disappear behind a distant set of waves.

I placed the miso bowl of kushi sauce by the soy sauce bottle near the sushi bar. Just then, Junichi-san flew towards me and grabbed the miso bowl by the bar and careened into the kitchen making guttural noises.

I yelled out to him, "Hey!!"

He didn't hear me or want to hear me. He took my sauce! I was just playing with it like every other kid would. I wasn't done with it! Great. Now how was I going to enjoy my kushi. I needed my sauce!

I peered through the noren curtains, looking for where he might have placed the bowl in hopes that I could get it back because if I ask for another miso bowl of kushi sauce, who knows what Junichi-san might do to it. I looked around in front of me and the only sauce I see is the soy sauce in the standard golden-labeled bottle. Not good enough. I need my miso bowl with kushi sauce.

Luke enters the garage to discover the roebots nowhere in sight. He takes a small controller from his utility belt similar to the one the Engawas were carrying. He activates the controller, which creates a low cracking sound of a wet towelette smacking glass, and Soy-3PO lets out a short yell and pops up from behind the Duskyhopper spacefish. He wobbles forward.

Luke asks, "What are you doing hiding there?"

Soy-3PO responds with concern, "It wasn't my fault, sir. Please don't empty me. I told him not to go, but he's faulty, moldy, malfunctioning; kept babbling and bubbling on about his mission." Luke cries out, "Oh no!"

Luke races out of the garage, followed by Soy-3PO, and searches the darkening horizon for the small bowl-shaped hydro-roebot. Soy-3PO struggles out of the homestead and onto the salt water edge as Luke scans the seascape with his electro-finoculars.

Soy-3PO breaks the tension by stating, "That Miso-D2 unit has always been a problem. These hydro-soyds are getting quite out of fin. Even I can't understand their logic at times." Luke replies in a frustrated voice, "How could I be so stupid? He's nowhere in sight. Blast it!" "Pardon me, sir, but couldn't we go after him?" "It's too dangerous with all the Clampeople around. We'll have to wait until morning." O-Ton yells up from the seaweed homestead plaza, "Luke, I'm shutting the power down for the night." Luke yells back, "All right, I'll be there in a few minutes."

He continues by muttering, "Minnow, am I gonna get it." Luke takes one final look across the darkening horizon but he sees nothing but wide open seas with a few waves cresting far off in the distance. He looks at Soy-3PO, "You know that little soyd is going to cause me a lot of trouble." Soy-3PO confirms, "Oh, he excels at that, sir. He tofully does."

I leaned forward, supporting my belly on the bar in front of me, and peered into the back of the kitchen. I was pretty sure I saw the miso bowl sitting by the sink. I wasn't entirely sure but it might be retrievable. Junichi-san was nowhere to be seen but I was pretty sure he was lurking about somewhere nearby, probably laughing because he took something I like. He had to know I wasn't finished.

Morning slowly creeps into the sparse but sparkling oasis of the sushi-made land that is the Katsu homestead. The serene views are suddenly broken by the yelling of Luke's Uncle O-Ton. His voice echoes throughout the seaweed island as he calls out for Luke. Luke is no where to be found. O-Ton returns to the homestead kitchen and asks Bifu if she has seen Luke this morning. She informs him that Luke said he had to do some things before he got started that day so he left early. She thinks that he left with the two new soyds and informs O-Ton about that as well. O-Ton is not very happy but hopes Luke will finish the work he needs him to do anyway before midday.

The waves and splashes of the raging ocean are a blur as Soy-3PO pilots the sleek trayspeeder gracefully across the vast sea. Luke leans over the back of the trayspeeder and adjusts something in the gill compartment. He fixes something and Soy-3PO signals that whatever was malfunctioning is now fine and Luke returns to the leading edge of the tray.

Luke looks over to Soy-3PO and says, "Old Zen Wasabi lives out in this direction somewhere, but I don't see how that Miso-D2 unit could have come this far. We must have missed him. Uncle O-Ton isn't going to take this very well."Soy-3PO responds, "Sir, would it help if you told him it was my fault?"Luke lights up and replies, "Sure. He needs you. He'd probably only empty you for a day or so…"

"Empty?! Well, uh, on the other fin if you hadn't removed his restraining towelette…"

Luke interrupts,"Wait, there's something dead ahead on the sonar scanner. It looks like our soyd...hit the accelerator."

Junichi-san suddenly leaped out from behind the curtains with a dish held high above his head. He spun around the curtain, almost gracefully. He brought the dish down to shoulder height and laid it before my mom.

As he placed the dish down, he glanced at my dad and yelled out, "Hokkigai!" Dad hadn't even noticed. My mom, with a somewhat horrified look upon her face, looked at my dad and back at Junichi-san and asked, "Hokey? He's not hokey!" As sweet as my mom usually is, she occasionally displays moments of what I'd call… extreme innocence… that usually borders on the verge of full out embarrassment. I did not know if she was trying to be funny or if she seriously thought that Junichi-san was calling dad hokey. Junichi-san just stood there nodding nervously, not understanding anything my mom said or implied. He had no idea what was happening. Hiroshi-san came to his rescue, half-dismissed him to the kitchen, and verified that the dish placed before my mom held hokkigai, surf clams. The surf clams were white with red tips and wrapped by a belt of dried seaweed. There were three on the plate. That meant I was going to be served at least one.

My mom started giggling at the situation and still did not reveal if she really understood that this dish was called hokkigai or if she thought Junichi-san was actually insulting her husband. She held up one hand and motioned to her belly with the other stating she couldn't possibly eat any more and motioned to my dad to take the dish. He was not paying attention. She then just placed the dish in front of me, assuming I would eat these after my kushi. She clearly has never paid attention to me or my eating habits at the sushi bar. Either that or she purposely ignored the fact that I do not eat sushi. I play with sushi. And besides, every piece of sushi served to me that night remained on my plate, uneaten or carried away hidden amongst the dishes. She didn't even seem to notice that.

From high on the crest of an ocean wave, the trayspeeder glides across the water's surface. Suddenly, two water-beaten Clampeople appear shrouded in their grimy seaweed. They peer over the edge of the waves. One of the creatures raises a long ominous laserbean rifle and points it at the trayspeeder but the second creature grabs the gun before it can be fired. The Clampeople, or Shucken Raiders as they're sometimes called, speak in a coarse, barbaric language as they get into an animated argument. The second Shucken Raider seems to get in the final word and the nomads scurry over the wavy surface.

I took two of the surf clams, the hokkigai, and placed them each on the wet towellete on the side of my plate that held the last fried tofu, the atsuage. I knew if my mom saw that, she'd get very upset. This stuff was not cheap or so I'm told every time we come here. I moved the soy sauce bottle close by the dish to hide the clams on the wet towelette. Before Hiroshi-san left to help other customers, I asked him if I might get back the miso bowl filled with katsu sauce that Junichi-san took away. I politely explained that I was not quite done with it. He smiled, glanced at Junichi-san with a frown, and bowed at me. He straightened a picture behind the bar of a man in scuba gear swimming near a large manta ray. Under the photo were the words "Manta birostris - Japan". I noticed that every time Hiroshi-san was upset, he adjusted or polished one of the many pictures that hung on the wall behind the bar.

The Shucken Raiders approach two large Mantas floating nearby, tied to a small seaweed-covered land mass. The monstrous, manta ray creatures are as large as whales, with huge lucid eyes on either side of their heads, tremendous cephalic lobes, and long, slimy, whip-like tails. The Shucken Raiders mount craddle-like saddles already strapped to the huge Mantas' slimy backs and ride off across and under the cresting waves.
The trayspeeder is floating on the surface of a massive lagoon, surrounded by steep piles of seaweed and a few operating land solidifiers. Luke, with his long laserbean rifle slung over his shoulder, stands before little Miso-D2.

Hiroshi-san returned with a miso bowl filled with katsu sauce and held it before me, not quite giving it to me. Maybe he was teasing me.

"Ok, here is katsu sauce, but do me favor and try eating the sushi. Ok?"

I fake smiled. Hiroshi-san picked up on this, sighed, and unceremoniously placed the bowl onto the bar in front of me. I shrugged.

Luke calls out to Miso-D2, "Hey, whoa, just where do you think you're going?"

Miso-D2 responds with feeble whistles as Soy-3PO confronts Miso-D2, "Master Luke here is your rightful owner. We'll have no more of this Obi-Wan Wasabi jibberish...and don't talk to me about your mission, either. You're fortunate he doesn't blast you into a million clay pieces right here."

A look of forgiveness takes over Luke as he instructs them, "Well, come on. It's getting late. I only hope we can get back before Uncle O-Ton really gets fried."

Soy-3PO recommends, "If you don't mind my saying so, sir, I think you should de-steam the little fugitive until you've gotten him back to your workshop."

Luke refuses, trusting Miso-D2 to not try anything further. Miso-D2 jumps to life suddenly with a barrage of frantic whistles and burps. Luke asks what is wrong with him.

Soy-3PO interprets, "Oh my...sir, he says there are several creatures approaching from the southeast.

Luke swings his rifle into position and looks to the south and exclaims, "Clampeople! Or worse! Come on, let's have a look. Come on."

I moved the two surf clams off of the wet naps and placed them on my plate behind the atsuage. I figured this way mom wouldn't bust me about playing with my food. The third surf clam was still on the serving dish. At least I'm doing something with some of these clams. Mom was stuffed and wouldn't touch them. Dad was sipping sake and engaged in deep conversation about Japanese baseball teams or something with some other regular customers and probably didn't even know the hokkigai dish was served to us. With all that, I was sure I would be lectured about playing with my food and how expensive sushi was.

Luke carefully makes his way to the top of a nearby wave crest and scans the calmer waters before him with his electro-finoculars. He spots two riderless Mantas. Soy-3PO struggles up behind the young adventurer, bobbing about in the choppy waves. Luke informs his companion that he spots two Mantas and, in fact, can see one of the Clampeople in the distance, bobbing along the surface.

Behind the bar, I saw Hiroshi-san take out some ginger root and clean it in the nearby sink. He chopped the scraggly pieces this way and that. He sliced thin pieces off and then started rolling them up together. He placed the thin slices into a jar filled with what looked like vinegar. He sealed the jar and placed it up high on a nearby shelf. He completely had my attention and seemed to know it. After placing the jar onto the shelf, he looked back at me, smiled, and said, "Gari. I'm making gari, pickled ginger root to clean your tastes between sushi dishes. You like?" He scraped the scraggly chopped up chunks and remnants of ginger root left over into his hand and threw them into a nearby trashcan. I must have been still watching intently. He grabbed another small ginger root scrap and gave it to me, nodding.

"Ginger, Billy-san. Good for man."

"Can I keep it, Hiroshi-san?" I asked.

"Why do you want to keep that? You cannot eat like that. I prepare for you."

"Uh, no. No, that's okay. I just want to... uh... smell it. Yeah, smell it. Seems fresh."

"Smell?! No taste?! Hmmph. Okay. I don't know why, but okay. It's okay. I don't need it. Maybe it will make you try my sushi, huh?!"

I looked around the room. With no one watching, I made small clubbing motions at the remaining atsuage on my plate with the small, scraggly ginger root. I hid this activity from mom and anyone else that might glance over at me by covering it with my other hand. The ginger root dented the fried tofu. I tucked the small root under the seaweed band that held the surf clam together.

Luke continues to watch the distant Shucken Raider through his electro-finoculars. Suddenly, something huge moves in front of his field of view. Before either Luke or Soy-3PO can react, a large, gruesome Shucken Raider looms over them. Soy-3PO is startled and backs away, and starts to sink in the choppy water. He can be heard gurgling and spitting for several moments as he dips, bobs and sinks down into the water. The towering Shucken Raider brings down his curved, double-pointed gari stick, the dreaded ginger weapon that has struck terror in the heart of the local settlers, cleansing tastes across the land-solidifier generated settlements. Luke manages to block the blow with his laserbean rifle, which is smashed to pieces which then immediately sink. The terrifried farm soy paddles backward until he is forced down the

31

crest of a very high wave. The sinister Shucken Raider floats above him on the wave crest with his gari weapon raised and lets out a horrible shriek.

Hiroshi-san returned to the bar in front of me and grabbed another root wrapped in a wet paper towel from the small refrigerator below the bar. He unwrapped the root and shaved off some of the outer skin and rinsed the root. He took out what appeared to be a cheese grater and placed it in one hand with the root in the other. He grated some of the green root off into a small dish using a circular motion and after a while formed a small pile of what I finally identified as wasabi. I never tried wasabi and didn't plan on ever trying wasabi.

Hiroshi-san looked at me as he wet a paper towel. He wrapped the remaining part of the root in the wet towel and placed the root into the refrigerator. He turned to me and showed me the contents in the small dish he had just prepared, leaving the grater for Junichi-san to pick up and clean in the kitchen.

"Wasabi, Billy-san! Sawa wasabi... from a fresh mountain stream in Japan. Friend in Nagano sent it to me. Very expensive."

I found this mildly amusing and asked, "Is it any good?" Hiroshi-san replied with a large smile on his face, "The best! I make for you if you try sushi?"

"Um... yeah, no thanks."

"Hmmm. Very sad. Very sad, indeed. Maybe someday soon?"

Hiroshi-san placed the small dish containing the fresh wasabi in front of my mom and asked her to taste it with the hokkigai and a little soy sauce. He showed her how to mix the wasabi in the soy sauce dish. She already knew how to do this. Hiroshi-san assumed her resistance to trying it right away was because she didn't understand how to eat it. She was just honestly full, I think. Either that or she doesn't like clams. Hiroshi-san left the prepared wasabi mixture by her plate and went to attend to another customer. My mom sniffed the mixture and jerked her head back ever so slightly signifying it might have been a bit too strong for her.

Miso-D2 forces himself under the leaves of a nearby clump of seaweed as the vicious Clampeople swim past carrying the limp Luke Soywalker, who is plopped into the water right before the trayspeeder. The Clampeople ransack the trayspeeder, throwing pieces and supplies in all directions. Suddenly they stop. Then, everything is quiet for a few moments. A great howling moan is heard echoing about the waves and nearby seaweed outcrops which sends the Clampeople fleeing in terror.

I took a small swatch of the wasabi near my mom's plate with my chopsticks and sculpted a small pile of it by the gari-damaged atsuage still on my dish.

Miso-D2 moves even tighter under the protection of the seaweed as the slight swishing sound that fryghtened off the Clampeople grows even closer, until a shredded, old green and pasty clump with discerning eyes appears and leans over Luke. His ancient white rice face, grated and weathered by exotic climates is set off by dark, penetrating eyes and a scraggly wasabi beard. Zen Wasabi squints his eyes as he scrutinizes the unconscious farm soy. Miso-D2 makes a slight gurgling sound and Zen turns and looks right at him.

Zen addresses the adrift soyd, "Hello there! Come here my little friend. Don't be afraid. Your miso is safe with me."

Miso-D2 streams over to where Luke lies half-sunken in a limp position and begins to whistle and burp his concern. Luke, disoriented, begins to come around.

Zen looks at Miso-D2 and comforts him by saying, "Don't worry, he'll be all right."

A stunned Luke, rubbing his dented brow, recovers a bit and asks, "What happened?"

"Rest easy, soy, you've had a busy day. You're fortunate you're still in one piece of tofu."

"Zen? Zen Wasabi! Minnow, am I glad to see you!"

"The Funamori waves are not to be traveled lightly. Tell me young Luke, what brings you out this far?"

Luke looks at Miso-D2 and states, "Oh, this little soyd! I think he's searching for his former master...I've never seen such devotion in a soyd before...there seems to be no stopping him. He claims to be the property of an Obi-Wan Wasabi. Is he a relative of yours? Do you know who he's talking about?" Zen ponders this for a moment, scratching his wasabi beard.

"Obi-Wan Wasabi...Obi-Wan? Now thats a name I haven't heard in a long time...a long time."

Luke adds, "I think my uncle knew him. He said he was cooked."

"Oh, he's not cooked, not...not yet."

"You know him!" "Well, of course, of course I know him. He's me! I haven't gone by the name Obi-Wan since oh, before you were a bean."

"Then the soyd does belong to you."

"Don't seem to remember ever owning a soyd. Very interesting..."

Zen Wasabi suddenly looks up at the overhanging wave crests. Zen cautions, "I think we better get indoors. The Clampeople are easily startled but they will soon be back and in greater numbers."

Luke sits up and shakes his soyhead and smooths out the tofu dents from the gari stick.

Miso-D2 lets out a pathetic gurgle causing Luke to remember something. He looks around.

Luke cries out, "Soy-3PO!"

I reached over to the small dish again to grab a little more wasabi since the pile on my plate was a little smaller than it should be. While reaching for the dish with my chopsticks, I accidentally knocked over the soy sauce bottle. The bottle hit the bar rather swiftly with a loud clink. The cap of the soy bottle chipped off and went flying somewhere onto the floor. Soy sauce started leaking out onto the bar. Mom jumped at the commotion. I panicked a little bit as I hurriedly picked up the soy sauce bottle and placed it upright.

Mom exclaimed, "Billy! What is wrong with you tonight, honey?!"

"I don't know. Sorry mom. I'll clean it up."

"Okay, try to calm down and just eat, ok? I hear the hokey clam stuff is really good."

I frowned.

She mopped up a little of the soy sauce with her wet towelette which, of course, didn't absorb much. I searched the floor for the cap and found it under mom's stool. It was a bit mangled. As I brought my head up over the bar, I saw Junichi-san staring at me with disapproving eyes, shaking his head. He was not happy that I almost broke one of his precious soy sauce bottles. He turned to my mom with a fake smile and nod, as he cleaned up the spill with a dish towel.

Little Miso-D2 floats at the top of a large wave crest looking down and begins to chatter away in whistles and beeps. Luke and Zen see a small soyl spill afloat on the surface of the ocean. They paddle over to a very scratched and oxidized Soy-3PO nearly fully submerged in the sea. His cap has broken off and is floating nearby, rusting. Luke tries to revive the inert roebot by shaking him and then pours a little soy into his damaged cap from a small vial in his utility belt. Soy-3PO shakes, rights himself in the water, and then revives in a very confused manner.

Stunned, Soy-3PO asks, "Where am I? I must have taken a bad dive..." Luke replies, "Can you float? We've got to get out of here before the Clampeople return." A dramatic Soy-3PO assesses and states, "I don't think I can make it. You go on, Master Luke. There's no sense in you risking yourself on my account. I'm done for... a lost soyl." Miso-D2 makes a burping sound. Luke scolds Soy-3PO, "No, you're not. What kind of talk is that?" Luke and Zen help the battered roebot to a stable floating position. Miso-D2 watches from the top of the wave crests. Zen glances around suspiciously. Sensing something, he swims up to the wave crest and sniffs the air. Zen informs, "Quickly, soy...they're on the move."

They make their way across the vast ocean to a small, floating seaweed-infested island, a place Zen Wasabi calls home.

Junichi-san took the soy sauce bottle with the mangled cap and my dish that still contained the damaged atsuage and some of the other uneaten items I collected from the evening. He took them into the kitchen and sat them by the edge of the sink, next to the grater Hiroshi-san used to make fresh wasabi. Chunks of grated wasabi still sat in the holes of the grater. Also by the sink was the first miso bowl still half-filled with kushi sauce that Junichi-san took from me earlier.

Luke Soywalker sits in the corner of a small seaweed home constructed on the small floating island, repairing Soy-3PO's cap. Zen Wasabi sits in the other corner of the small home, deep in thought.

Luke continues the conversation by informing, "No, my father didn't fight in the Sushi Wars. He was a navigator on a spice spacefish freighter."

Zen replies, "That's what your uncle told you. He didn't hold with your father's ideals. Thought he should have stayed here and not gotten involved."

Luke, curiously excited, asked, "You fought in the Kamaboko Wars?"

"Yes, I was once a Red-Eye Knight, the same as your father." "I wish I'd known him."

"He was the best spacefish pilot in the galaxsea, and a cunning warrior. I understand you've become quite a good pilot yourself. And he was a good friend. Which reminds me..."

Zen gets up and goes to a chest where he rummages around. As Luke finishes repairing Soy-3PO's cap and starts to fit the restraining towelette back on, Soy-3PO looks at him nervously. Luke thinks about the towelette for a moment then puts it on the napkin. Zen shuffles up and presents Luke with two short findles, each with several buttons on it.

Zen starts, "I have something here for you. Your father wanted you to have this when you were old enough, but your uncle wouldn't allow it. He feared you might follow old Obi-Wan on some fool idealistic crusade like your father did."

Soy-3PO asks to rest for a while and Luke agrees. Zen Wasabi gives Luke the weapon.

Luke inspects it and asks, "What is it?"

"Your father's chopsabers. This is the weapon of a Red-Eye Knight. Not as clumsy or as random as a laserbean blaster. Hold it by the findles there."

Luke pushes a button on the findles. Two long, thin sticks of light shoot out about three inches and flicker there, emanating from each findle. The light plays across the seaweed ceiling.

Zen continues, "An elegant weapon for a more civilized time. For over a thousand generations the Red-Eye Knights were the guardians of peace, good sushi and justice in the Old Sushi Republic, before the dark times, before the Tempura."

Luke hasn't really been listening, too enamored by the lure of the chopsabers and the adventures they represent.

Junichi-san exited the kitchen and went to a back storage room on the other side of the sushi bar. He returned momentarily with a large sack of rice slung over his shoulder. As he passed by, he glanced at my dishes. I wasn't sure if he was looking for more evidence of me playing with my food or if he was just so heavily programmed to clear dishes that are empty that he was scouting the barscape as part of his routine.

Luke still gazing at the chopsabers, asks "How did my father spoil?"

Zen Wasabi pauses for a moment and then says "A young Red-Eye named Squid Vader, who was a pupil of mine until he turned to evil, helped the Tempura hunt down and destroy the Red-Eye Knights. He betrayed and cooked your father. Now the Red-Eye are all but extinct. Vader was seduced by the dark side of the Rice, the Brown Rice."

"The Rice?"

Zen explains, "Well, the Rice is what gives a Red-Eye his power. It's an energy grass field created by living things. It surrounds us and penetrates us. It binds the galaxsea together... because it's sticky!"

Junichi-san returned after dropping off the rice in the kitchen and cleared some empty dishes.

Miso-D2 interrupts the conversation by burping.

Zen turns and looks at Miso-D2 and addresses him. "Now, let's see if we can't figure out what you are, my little friend, and where you come from."

Luke tries to explain to Zen about how he saw part of the message contained within Miso-D2 but is cut short as the recorded image of the beautiful young Rebel Princess Maki is projected from Miso-D2's main bowl.

The rollogram of Princess Maki informs, "General Wasabi, years ago you served my father in the Kamaboko Wars. Now he begs you to help him in his struggle against the Tempura. I regret that I am unable to present my father's request to you in person, but my spacefish has fallen under attack and I'm afraid my mission to bring you to Abaloneraan has failed. I have placed information vital to the survival of the Rebellion into the data seed systems of this Miso-D2 unit. My father will know how to retrieve it. You must see this soyd safely delivered to him on Abaloneraan. This is our most desperate hour. Help me, Obi-Wan Wasabi, you're my only hope."

Junichi-san grabbed the sprayer from the sink and rinsed off all of the dishes he had collected.

There is a little static on the rollogram of Princess Maki and the tidemission is cut short. Old Zen leans back and scratches his wasabi beard. He silently puffs on a tarnished chrome water pipe. Luke has plates in his eyes.

Zen Wasabi seems convicted and informs Luke, "You must learn the ways of the Rice if you're to come with me to Abaloneraan."

Luke, laughing, responds, "Abaloneraan? I'm not going to Abaloneraan. I've got to go home. It's late. I'm in for it as it is."

Zen counters, "I need your help, Luke. She needs your help. I'm getting too old for this sort of thing."

"I can't get involved! I've got work to do! It's not that I like the Tempura. I hate it! But there's nothing I can do about it right now. It's such a long way from here."

Zen advises, "That's your uncle talking."

Luke realizing he is in serious trouble with his uncle wonders how he is ever going to explain this.

"Learn about the Rice, Luke."

"Look, I can take you as far as Anchoviehead. You can get a traysport there to Mos Iceley or wherever you're going." Zen smiles and replies, "You must do what you feel is right, of course."

3 THE DEATH STARFISH

It was becoming a very late night and my parents were not showing any signs of wrapping this dinner up. My mom was hiding yawns in her wet nap after slurping some engawa leftover in front of her. My dad was still engaged in conversations about Japan with the nearby customer that, by either good or bad luck, sat by my dad this evening for dinner. Such was the risk of sitting at the sushi bar.

My father had a fair amount of sake to drink and showed signs of being overly happy, maybe even a little tipsy. He erupted in laughter over his neighboring sushi bar mate's last comment that no else seem to hear. He slapped the back of this poor man, smiled and raised his drink. My mother was fighting to stay in the conversation enough to support my dad when he needed it with a chuckle, a nod, or remembering some insignificant fact that supported his in-progress story. She tried to be a good wife for him whenever possible, or at least, whenever convenient.

My dad continued to celebrate stories with the older Japanese man sitting by him as fearlessness seemed to grow within him. He raised his hand as he gazed eagerly across the sushi bar at Hiroshi-san. He waved him over as soon as Hiroshi-san made eye contact.

My dad addressed Hiroshi-san and said, "My good man, Hiroshi-san, I would like something exotic to eat, something neither of us have ever had. My treat!" He looked towards his new friend and glanced back at my mom as if to ask, "this is ok, right?"

Hiroshi-san thought about options for a few seconds. His eyes squinted in thought and then settled on the back wall of the sushi restaurant.

"Ah... I think I have something most special, most exotic. Not even too expensive, but very unique. Not for an American, maybe?", said Hiroshi-san.

"Perfect!", my dad yelled out.

"Ok, then. I will bring you the Starfish Surf Special!"

"Starfish wha?!", replied my dad with a puzzled look worn on his face.

My dad's new friend shrugged his shoulders as my dad glanced at him. The old man seemingly didn't understand what was going on, exactly. Hiroshi-san entered the kitchen. My dad smiled at the old man and also shrugged.

Somewhere, in the oceanverse, an Imperial Stargazer approaches an evil-looking, plate-sized starfish battle station known as the Death Starfish. The armored starfish battle station is enormous and made from very advanced bio-materials. It floats in orbit around a nearby plate. It is grey in color and immense with its five arms sprawling from the core of the battle station. In the center is a very large circular dish, a five-point focal laserbean weapon, thought to be the most powerful weapon in the galaxsea. The Death Starfish is thought to have enough power to destroy an entire tide pool or stack of plates.

Hiroshi-san scurried over to a special refrigeration box by the back wall of the sushi bar. He searched inside and pulled out a container that frosted over almost immediately. He instructed Junichi-san to get a pot of water boiling immediately. Junichi-san scampered into the kitchen, to the stove, and fired up a pot of water. Once the water was boiling, Junichi-san called over Hiroshi-san. He inspected the pot's contents and smelled the steam. He added a teaspoon of salt to the boiling water, opened the recently defrosted container and pulled out a surprisingly large starfish that crinkled its arms within his grip. Hiroshi-san placed the suspended starfish in the water and replaced the pot's cover before tending to another customer.

Four minutes later, Hiroshi-san returned to the pot and removed the starfish from the boiling water and placed the starfish in a bowl of cold water for 15 seconds, that he counted off in Japanese looking at the ceiling. He removed the starfish, dried it off, and placed it in the center of a long ironwood board with a pair of special pliers used to crack the hard outer shell. The "meat" of the starfish must have been difficult to get to.

He then grabbed some fresh tuna from the nearest icebox and placed it in a shallow pan over the same stove and seared it. Once done, he placed the tuna next to the starfish on the ironwood serving tray. He prepared some sea bream whitefish sushi and placed that around the starfish. Finally, he prepared some salmon roe and sculpted it into an ambiguous form held together by seaweed and placed that on the other side of the starfish. Hiroshi-san decorated the ironwood tray further with

39

some random cabbage shreddings and other unidentifiable radish-like items. He proudly delivered the finished serving tray to the sushi bar in front of my dad and his new friend. My mom curiously looked over my father's shoulder, probably wondering how much that dish is going to cost them.

"Here's the special one!", said Hiroshi-san to my dad as he winked.

Inside the control center of the Death Starfish, eight Imperial seanators and generals sit around a black conference napkin. Imperial saketroopers stand guard around the room. Clammander Tataki, a young, thin, slightly seared, and yet slimy-looking vinegary tuna general, is speaking.

"Until this starfish battle station is fully operational, we are vulnerable. The Rebel Alliance is too well equipped. They're more dangerous than you realize."

The bitter Admiral Madai, a stark and stench-filled snapper admiral, twists nervously in his chair and chimes in,"Dangerous to your spacefish fleet, Clammander Tataki, not to this starfish battle station!" Tataki rebukes, "The Rebellion will continue to gain support in the Imperial Seanate as long as..."

Suddenly, Clammander Tataki's speech is cut short as everyone turns to see Grand Moff Tarako, the ambiguously shaped pollack roe governor of the Imperial outland regions, enter. He is followed by his powerful ally, The Surf Lord, Squid Vader. All of the generals stand and bow before the evil-looking, thinly ambiguous governor as he takes his place at the head of the napkin. The Dark Lord stands behind him, black tentacles swimming about his immensely intimidating frame.

Grand Moff Tarako interrupts the silence, "The Imperial Seanate will no longer be of any concern to us. I've just received word that the Tempuraror has dissolved the council permanently. The last remnants of the Old Republic have been sunk away."

Clammander Tataki responds, "That's impossible! How will the Tempuraror maintain control without the bureaucracy?"

"The regional governors now have direct control over territories. Fear will keep the local tidal zones in line. Fear of this starfish battle station," replies Tarako.

Tataki worriedly continues, "And what of the Rebellion? If the Rebels have obtained a complete menu of this starfish battle station it is possible, however unlikely, that they might find a weakness and exploit it."

Squid Vader slides forward a bit and informs, "The plans you refer to will soon be back in our possession."

Admiral Midai confidently informs, "Any attack made by the Rebels against this starfish would be a useless gesture, no matter what menu data they've obtained. This starfish is now the ultimate power in the oceanverse. I suggest we use it!"

My dad eyed the ironwood tray over inspecting the various items as he peered over his nose and uttered "hmmm" or "huh" under his breath every time his eye passed over the greyish-brown starfish in the center. He looked for something familiar, something he felt he could digest initially on this exotic plate that he himself had requested. The thought itself seemed sobering. After confirming his choice, he proudly grabbed his chopsticks from aside his plate, evened out the lengths by banging them on the sushi bar in front of him, and aggressively snagged the whitefish, inspected it closely, and dunked it in the tiny dish of soy sauce. Then, just as he was about to place the sushi into his mouth, he glanced over at the old man next to him that he had just befriended and paused. Realizing he had likely made a cultural mistake by not offering his new friend something from the tray first, he awkwardly eased the soy-sopped whitefish from near his mouth towards the old man's face, gently jumping it into the air as if to ask the old man, "you want this piece right here?" The old man, with horrifiedly raised eyebrows, pushed a grin onto his face despite his strong inclination to show displeasure. My father, continuing to flub, raised the sad-looking, squished and dripping whitefish and said "Okey, dokey!" as he plopped it into his own mouth.

Squid Vader, seeing undue arrogance in Admiral Midai, scolds, "Don't be too proud of this delectable terror you've constructed. The ability to destroy a plate is insignificant next to the power of the Rice." Admiral Midai replies, "Don't try to fryghten us with your saucerer's ways, Squid Vader. Your sad devotion to that ancient starch has not helped you conjure up the stolen dataseeds, or given you clairvoyance enough to find the Rebel's hidden plate..."

Suddenly, Midai chokes, gasps and starts to turn brown and spoil under Squid Vader's spell.

Squid Vader states, "I find your lack of carbohydrates disturbing." Grand Moff Tarako interrupts, "Enough of this! Squid Vader, release him!"

"As you wish. I won't snapper his neck...this time."

"This bickering is pointless. Squid Vader will provide us with the location of the Rebel secret plate by the time this starfish is operational. We will then crush the Rebellion with one swift wave, like a tsunami."

Junichi-san quickly scurried out of the kitchen with a bucket of clams as he glanced in awe at the Starfish Surf Special. He had clearly not ever seen this dish served before. My dad checked the sake bottle near the starfish dish to see if it was empty. It wasn't. My dad then reached for the special pliers intended for use on the starfish and inspected them. He clearly wasn't sure what they were for as he exercised the tool. He playfully brought them near my mom's face, pretending to squish her nose. She was clearly annoyed but stayed somewhat tolerant and let out a fake giggle as she looked over at the neighboring old man, slightly embarrassed. My dad was officially tipsy. Great, too much sake. Junichi-san made his way back to the kitchen carrying a destroyed crab carcass and some silver shell cracking tools on a large, dirty serving dish. Someone at the other end of the sushi bar clearly liked to eat crab and was quite thorough in doing just that.

Meanwhile, an Imperial Gai Fighter, a fast spacefish made from a separated clam used by the Tempura to battle dogfish style, races toward the Death Starfish.

Two saketroopers open the pore to the digestive gland currently holding Princess Maki prisoner and allow several Imperial guards to enter. Princess Maki's face is filled with defiance, which slowly gives way to fear as a giant torture crab enters, followed by Squid Vader.

Squid Vader begins, "And now, your Gai-ness, we will discuss the location of your hidden Rebel plate."

The torture crab gives off a steady hissing sound as it approaches Princess Maki and extends one of its armor-clad arms bearing a large claw, ready to pinch and strangle the truth out of the princess. The digestive gland pore slides shut and the long digestive gland prisoner block hallway appears peaceful as the muffled screams of the Rebel princess are barely heard by anyone.

My father shrugged his shoulders at the special pliers in his hand. It didn't occur to him at all that they might be needed to actually eat something on the Starfish Surf Special dish. He placed the pliers on the edge of the bar. He then returned his attention to the old man sitting next to him, clearly trying to finish his dinner and escape this elongated conversation. My father encouraged the old man to take what he wanted from the Starfish Surf Special and really tried to offer him the starfish in particular. As he turned to the old man, my dad knocked the pliers onto the ground. The old man gave in and gently took a piece of the seared, vinegary tuna, dabbed it in his soy sauce dish, and ate it while overtly nodding his thanks to my father as graciously as he could. My father continued to push the starfish onto his new friend, probably mostly because he wasn't sure how to eat it and was hoping the old man would demonstrate. He didn't. Each time my father motioned to the starfish, the old man would wince and say "No, thank you. For you, special one."

Junichi-san came back out of the kitchen carrying an empty bucket and eyed the Starfish yet again in disbelief. He shook his puzzled head as he scampered off. Minutes later, he returned to the kitchen with a bucketful of empty and separated clam shells, still eyeing the starfish.

Again, several Gai Fighters approach the Death Starfish.

Inside the control room of the Death Starfish, Squid Vader addresses Grand Moff Tarako, "Her resistance to the mind crab claw is considerable. It will be some time before we can extract any information from her."

An Imperial seigo officer interrupts the meeting, "The final check-out is complete. All systems are operational. What main course shall we set?"

Tarako muses, "Perhaps she would respond to an alternative form of persuasion."

Squid Vader curiously asks, "What do you mean?"

"I think it is time we demonstrate the full power of this starfish."

Tarako orders an Imperial seigo soldier to set course for Princess Maki's home plate of Abaloneraan.

The night was dragging on and Junichi-san was very busily cleaning surfaces and collecting items from behind the bar, placing them into storage compartments behind the bar. As I watched him, he would occasionally glance over his shoulder in my direction, pretending to look beyond me, probably to see if I was watching him. This somehow seemed to make him nervous.

Hiroshi-san came out from behind the bar and went to the restaurant front door and flipped the "Open" sign around. He was closing the restaurant to new customers. Ordinarily, this would be good news, but because my parents come here so often, Hiroshi-san lets them stay until he is absolutely ready to close for the night. So, while they cleaned, we sat at the bar, me bored out of my skull and my parents ensnaring lingering customers into their conversational web.

Hiroshi-san yelled out something to Junichi-san in Japanese and I had no idea what it meant.

Junichi-san immediately stopped placing items away, pulled out a serving tray, and went to the ice box display in front of me. He opened the latched door on the other side of the bar and, one by one, took out some abalone resting in the ice and placed them onto the tray. He made a circle on the tray out of eight abalone half-shells.

Abaloneraan looms behind the Death Starfish battle station. Admiral Midai enters the quiet brain control room and bows before Governor Tarako, who stands before the huge wall membrane displaying a small green plate. Admiral Midai confirms their location in the Abaloneraan tidal zone. Squid Vader and two saketroopers enter the control room with Princess Maki, her roll body bound with soba noodles.

Princess Maki recognizes Tarako and addresses him with contempt, "Governor Tarako, I should have expected to find you holding Squid Vader's leash. I recognized your foul stench when I was brought on board."

Tarako replies, "Charming to the last. You don't know how hard I found it signing the order to cook your life!"

"I'm surprised you had the courage to take the responsibility yourself!"

"Princess Maki, before your searing execution, I would like you to be my guest at a ceremony that will make this battle starfish operational. No tidal zone will dare oppose the Tempuraror now."

"The more you tighten your grip, Tarako, the more tidal zones will slip through your roe."

"Not after we demonstrate the power of this starfish. In a way, you have determined the choice of the plate that'll be destroyed first. Since you are reluctant to provide us with the location of the secret Rebel plate, I have chosen to test this starfish's destructive power...on your home plate of Abaloneraan."

"No! Abaloneraan is peaceful. We have no weapons. We're just slimy goop in a pretty shell. You can't possibly..."

"You would prefer another target? A military target? Then name the tidal zone!"

Tarako waves some of his seaweed menacingly toward Princess Maki.

"I grow tired of asking this. So it'll be the last time. Where is the Rebel secret plate?"

Princess Maki overhears an intercom voice announcing the approach to Abaloneraan. She hangs her nori and utters softly in defeat, "Pantooine. They're on Pantooine."

"There. You see Squid Vader, she can be reasonable."

Tarako addresses Midai, "Continue with the operation. You may fire when ready."

Princess Maki, distraught in shock, yells out, "What?!"

"You're far too trusting. Pantooine is too remote to make an effective demonstration. But don't worry. We will deal with your Rebel friends soon enough."

Princess Maki screams, "No!"

My father, not to be shown up by his own ordering of exotic food, decided to try to eat the starfish. His pride drove his hunger. He looked around and then tried to grab the starfish with his chopsticks. The starfish was too heavy for his grip and it started to fall as he brought it closer to his mouth. Then gravity completely took over and the starfish slipped through my father's chopsticks and fell toward his plate and small dish of soy sauce. He panicked, dropped his chopsticks and quickly tried to catch the starfish with his left hand. When his hand came across the bar, it hit the sake bottle onto the plate making a loud clatter. He threw his right hand to catch the sake bottle and slapped the starfish toward the ice box. The starfish went flying across the bar and smashed into the tray of abalone. The abalone went flying across the back of the bar and slammed into the back wall. Junichi-san ducked out of the way from the flying half-shells and slipped on the damp floor. He landed outright on his back with a cracking sound as the abalone half-shells pelted him in the face and stomach. The abalone half-shells sat scattered on the floor, all of them open-shell down. The tray was splintered into many pieces scattered along the floor.

Squid Vader clammands, "Commence primary bean ignition."
A button is pressed which switches on a panel of lights in the Death Starfish brain control room. A hooded Imperial seigo soldier reaches overhead and pulls a nerve lever. Another nerve lever is pulled. Squid Vader reaches for still another nerve lever and a bank of pulses on a control panel and nearby wall light up. Five huge laserbeans emanate from within the outer dish area on the Death Starfish and converge in to a single laserbean that lashes out toward Abaloneraan. The small green plate of Abaloneraan blows up into fractions of goopy shell dust instantaneously.

Hiroshi-san, still by the front door, ran over to see what the commotion was and completely blamed Junichi-san for dropping the abalone onto the floor. In half-Japanese, half-English, he scolded Junichi-san about not having any abalone now for what I assumed was tomorrow's special green soup. Junichi-san rose to his feet, started to open his mouth, but decided simply to bow furiously and began cleaning up the mess. He threw the abalone half-shells into the trash can and sighed heavily, throwing evil glances my way occasionally as he rubbed his back. Not sure what I did here!? Why was he mad at me? Ok, so inside, I was laughing a little bit but I was very sure I didn't let out even one squeak or smirk. My dad had his head in his hands in disgust, moaning "No, no, no!" My mom started apologizing to everyone, even some of the last remaining customers on the other side of the restaurant.

Hiroshi-san apologized to her as he handed her the check with a stern frown.

4 MOS ICELY CANNEDTUNA

There were bits and pieces of various sushi pretty much all over the bar and floor after the starfish disaster. My father became very apologetic and was chipping away at his embarrassment by explaining to everyone within ear shot of how the starfish was too heavy for wooden chopsticks and if he had metal ones it wouldn't have "gotten away". He continued with some poor and desperate fishing jokes and something about how maybe the starfish wasn't quite yet dead and leapt off his chopsticks. Hiroshi-san was losing his patience with the whole scene, taking it all out on Junichi-san, mostly because it meant more clean-up time was necessary and he didn't want to further upset a very good customer.

Junichi-san was clearly upset. He shook his head side to side as he started to clear the bar in front of us of leftover sushi remnants. There were tiny bits of food here and there about the bar that Junichi-san tried to scoop up with a towel. There were turned over dishes, knocked over bottles, spilled sauces, and random bits of the various sushi my parents ordered throughout the night. I decided to kill time by poking the various shrapnel with the leftover piece of ginger root Hiroshi-san gave me. This annoyed Junichi-san. He motioned towards me with the towel as if to slap my hand away but never made contact. I smiled. He sneered. Most importantly, this meant I didn't have to eat any sushi. Brilliantly tragic.

Luke Soywalker and Zen Wasabi speed across the vast ocean after their intense discussion about Luke's father and the ways of the Rice. The trayspeeder stops before what remains of the huge Engawas' traysport, oddly half afloat and slightly listing before a small land-solidified island. Luke and Zen carefully swim among the flotsam and jetsam torn from the traysport and discover floating bodies of Engawa,

47

fried and scattered near a small outcropping of seaweed by the small island beach.

Luke breaks the silent awe, "It looks like Clampeople did this, all right. Look, here are Gari sticks floating about and Manta bites out of the seaweed. It's just... I've never heard of them attacking anything this big before."

Zen closely inspects the seaweed and comments, "They didn't. But we are meant to think they did. These bites are clearly bottle or sushi made. Mantas do indeed have teeth but they are like pin heads, small and nearly 300 or so in number. They filter their food through their gills. They do not bite."

Luke further observes, "These are the same Engawas that sold us Miso-D2 and Soy-3PO."

"And these laserbean blast points, too accurate for Clampeople. Only Imperial saketroopers are so precise," adds Zen.

"Why would Imperial troops want to slaughter Engawas?"

Luke looks back at Miso-D2 and Soy-3PO who are inspecting the fried Engawas and it occurs to him that if the saketroopers have learned who the Engawas sold the soyds to, then that would lead them to his home. With this sudden and horrible realization, Luke swims quickly for the trayspeeder and jumps in.

Zen calls out, "Wait, Luke! It's too dangerous. You could get beaned!"

Junichi-san shook his head as he collected toppled bottles and dishes hurriedly onto his tray. I decided I had better not push my luck with Junichi-san any more so I focused my attention on eating my kushi, which luckily survived. I was still a bit hungry and I needed to distract myself away from what Junichi-san was doing. The only problem was that my kushi was cold. I barely like kushi and cold kushi is just not very good. I called over to Hiroshi-san since I didn't want to bother Junichi-san. He seemed like he was about to lose it.

"Hiroshi-san! Hiroshi-san, could you please heat up my kushi?"

Hiroshi-san came over, sighed with a forced smile, seemed very upset, and took my plate with two pieces of kushi left into the kitchen. I heard him open the microwave door, place the dish in, and hit a bunch of buttons with beeps. He grunted. More beeps. He grunted again, this time with a questioning tone. More grunt and beeps were emitted. The microwave started and Hiroshi-san ran back out of the kitchen through the noren curtains shaking his head, visibly frustrated.

A few minutes went by and the microwave was still running. I became a little concerned about my kushi getting too hot and overcooked so I called over for Hiroshi-san but he was at the other end of the restaurant clearing another table. I called again but he did not hear me. Junichi-san was my only hope.

"Junichi-san? Can you please check my kushi? It seems like it has been cooking for a long time."

"Huh? You what want...kushi?"

"In the microwave. It is still cooking. I can hear the meat sizzling."

"What sizz... ing mean?"

"Kushi! It's burning!"

"Huh? Burning?! What burn?"

I pointed to the kitchen. Junichi-san looked into the kitchen and saw smoke come from the microwave. He dropped the towel onto the bar and scurried into the kitchen, stopped the microwave, and opened the door. Smoke started puffing out of the kitchen. Junichi-san came out of the kitchen with two completely blackened and charred pieces of curled up kushi, still smoldering.

Junichi-san looked at me blankly, trying to form words, and finally said, "Ah... no good, huh? Hiroshi-san cook too much. Hmmm. You want?"

He waved away the smoke rising off my charred kushikatsu.

Luke races off in the battered trayspeeder across the sea, leaving Zen and the two roebots alone with the smoldering, listing Engawa traysport. The trayspeeder roars up to the homestead on the land-solidified island and the structures are burning. Luke jumps out and waddles to the smoking remnants on the land that was once his home. Debris is scattered everywhere and it looks as if a great battle has taken place.

Luke cries out, "Uncle O-Ton! Aunt Bifu! Uncle O-Ton!"

Luke waddles about in a daze looking for his aunt and uncle. Suddenly, he comes upon their smoldering remains. O-Ton Katsu and Bifu Katsu are pork and beef slabs, charred beyond recognition, blackened, ashen, curled and still sizzling. Luke Soywalker is stunned and cannot speak. Hate replaces fear and a new resolve comes over him.

I shook my head in disappointment and showed my anger. My kushi was completely inedible. There was no way to eat this charred mass of meat on my plate. Junichi-san looked at me and shrugged his shoulders. He could have cared less but it would be hard for him to do so. I sneered at the plate and waved it away. I was officially a dissatisfied customer and had my father not created a huge mess, I would have asked for another order of kushi. Junichi-san shrugged at me and took the dish back into the kitchen and emptied it into the trash. He came back to the sushi bar and grabbed his towel and collected more remnants on the bar onto a chipped dish. He returned to the kitchen and scraped the plate into the sink, turned on the water, and then turned on the garbage disposal. A loud chopping sound emerged from the kitchen for a minute or so and then faded away as the motor slowed to a halt, water still running.

Luke returns to the small island site where he left Zen and the soyds. There is a large grating sound coming from the Engawa traysport. As Luke approaches, he sees the Engawa bodies fed into a grinder by the roebots on the broken traysport with the small chopped up bits and pieces falling into the water. Luke stops the trayspeeder in front of Zen Wasabi. Luke realizes the Engawa bits will now feed other animals in the sea as he watches the bits float away with the tides. The occasional remnant gets chomped by unseen creatures beneath the surface.

Zen speaks, "There's nothing you could have done, Luke, had you been there. You'd have been fried too and the soyds would be in the fins of the Tempura."

Luke, angry, replies, "I want to come with you to Abaloneraan. There's nothing here for me now. I want to learn the ways of the Rice and become a Red-Eye like my father."

Junichi-san continued to clear dishes and carried them to the kitchen.

Luke, Miso-D2, Soy3-PO, and Zen Wasabi load into the trayspeeder and head north across the sea. The trayspeeder floats atop a large wave crest overlooking the oceanport Mos Icely. Luke and Zen exit to scout out the view. It is a haphazard array of low, grey, shell structures and semi-domes on a large land-solidified island. A harsh wind rushes across the crew of the trayspeeder which reminds them of the harsher conditions and temperatures at Mos Icely.

Zen says, "Mos Icely Oceanport. You will never find a more wretched cesspool of scad and villainy. We must be cautious... and don't fall into the sea foam. It's gross."

Zen looks over at Luke, who gives the old Red-Eye a determined smile. Before them lies a stagnation pool in the ocean, hot, odiferous and filled with strange seaweed of wild varieties holding afloat various structures that house the evils of travelers from afar amidst a vast stench of stagnant sea foam.

My mother, having witnessed most of the kushi-destruction events, began haggling with Junichi-san. She pleaded that because the kushi was destroyed, her son didn't have a proper meal. And with that, she stated, she should not have to pay for the kushikatsu. Junichi-san looked out of the corners of his eyes and felt a wave of nervousness overcome him. He frantically searched the room with darting eyes for Hiroshi-san without moving his face. Junichi-san, on a good day, would have understood every other word from my fast-talking, english-speaking mother. Today was not a good day for him. My mother became aware that Junichi-san understood little of what she had said. She looked at the sushi bar in front of her, looked at my dad, and sighed heavily, realizing that my father had been responsible for more damage than the kushi incident. She shrugged her shoulders and gave Junichi-san her credit card with the check. Junichi-san hesitantly took the card and looked around wondering what he should do.

The trayspeeder is stopped on a crowded bed of seaweed by several combat-ready saketroopers. The saketroopers look over the two soyds in the back of the trayspeeder.

One of the saketroopers asks Luke, "How long have you had these soyds?"

Luke, with confidence, responds, "About three or four fishing seasons."

Zen leans over toward Luke's side of the trayspeeder and offers, "They're for sale if you want them."

Hiroshi-san was no where in sight. Junichi-san decided to run the check with the credit card he was given. Junichi-san went to the sales terminal and punched in the cost of the meal and swiped the credit card. The machine asked for verification. Junichi-san punched in some numbers as he inspected the card. The machine beeped at him. He looked at the card and came back to my mom.

"Card uh... no work. Need new card," he said to my mom.

My mom looked puzzled, took the card back, saw that it had expired, and slapped my dad on the arm.

She held her hand out and addressed my dad, "Tom, your card. Mine is expired. Did we get new ones in the mail?"

My dad, still in a bit of a haze, reached into his pocket somewhat confused and threw his wallet in front of my mom onto the sushi bar figuring this would get him out of any potential trouble he might have gotten into with her. She looked at him somewhat disgusted. The good-wife show she put on for the fellow customers and my dad all night long eroded instantly. She was greatly annoyed.

She waved the wallet at Junichi-san and said "You don't need my card any more."

"I don't need your card now?" asked Junichi-san, very puzzled.

My mom replied, "Nope. That is not the payment you are looking for. This is."

She pulled out a small wad of cash from my father's wallet.

"Better for your business, Junichi-san," she continued with a smirk.

There was a small look of satisfaction that emerged onto my mother's face as she emptied my dad's wallet of cash. She grabbed my dad's hand and slapped the much thinner wallet into his palm. He replaced the wallet back into his pocket, fairly oblivious to the fact that it now weighed significantly less.

The saketrooper addresses Luke Soywalker, still sitting in the stopped trayspeeder.

"Let me see your identifincation."

Luke becomes very nervous as he fumbles to find his identifincation while Zen Wasabi speaks to the saketrooper in a very controlled voice.

"You don't need to see his identifincation," says Zen.

The saketrooper responds, "We don't need to see his identifincation."

Zen continues, "These are not the soyds you're looking for."

The saketrooper, in a drone-like voice, replies, "These are not the soyds we are looking for."

Zen, waving a small piece of white rice before the saketrooper, evenly states, "He can go about his business."

The saketrooper continues, "You can go about your business."

Zen addresses Luke, "Roll along."

The saketrooper motions for the trayspeeder to advance and impatiently says, "Roll along. Roll along."

Junichi-san took the cash, counted it and returned the change to my mom. My mom, clearly in charge of the situation, placed a generous tip on the sushi bar and apologized for the mess her husband made. She began to pack up her things. My dad was swaying back and forth on the sushi bar stool. He was still awake but probably not feeling very good.

Junichi-san bowed and accepted the tip. He continued to wipe down the sushi bar. Hiroshi-san returned from the back room and began to see if everything was ok after the evening's incident. She nodded her approval and apologized once again as she rose from her stool. She helped my dad to his feet and called back to me to get ready to go.

As I started to get up, I realized I didn't actually want to leave. This was a first. What would become of the sushi after I left the sushi bar? These raw pieces of fish now had meaning to me. They were, dare I say, fun. Sure, they still tasted horrible, probably, but they had... they had... a life now! I realized I had something to return to next time we came to the sushi bar. I still hated the taste of sushi but now I had a destiny to fulfill on behalf of all sushiforms. I pushed in my stool underneath the bar slowly and waved goodbye to Junichi-san. He nodded without really looking my way and started wrapping the leftover fish and other food items from that evening and placed them inside the refrigerator. Not having seen the inside of the refrigerator, I could only imagine what strange things my sushi friends could encounter.

Junichi-san returned and placed the surviving leftover food he took from my dish, my atsuage, a piece of engawa, and the wad of fresh wasabi, into a clear, plastic to-go container. Hiroshi-san, feeling sorry about the starfish incident and the kushi destruction, brought out another clear, plastic to-go container containing a large veggie roll encased in extra seaweed, some yellowfish sushi, and an order of rainbow fish sushi. He explained that he prepared these items for us since much of our food ended up on the floor and was just in case we got hungry on the subway ride home.

My mother nodded her thanks. My father bowed and apologized yet again. We then slowly headed for the exit as my parents were still talking with Hiroshi-san. I decided to carry the to-go boxes for my mom. Junichi-san returned to the refrigerator and opened it up wide. All I saw were very large and strange wrappings and containers of raw fish of various types. Junichi-san placed a chunk of fresh tuna into a container and loaded it into the refrigerator. I looked down at my to-go box, which I mistakenly held at an angle, and saw the engawa and the atsuage rolling around in the container. Junichi-san grabbed the soy sauce bottles from around the bar and started placing them on the shelf.

The trayspeeder pulls up in front of a rundown circular tin structure on the outskirts of the Oceanport that had the word "CannedTuna" roughly painted on the side. Various strange forms of traysports, including several unusual fish of burden, are docked outside the CannedTuna bar. An Engawa swims up and begins to fondle the trayspeeder.

Soy-3PO looks upon the Engawa in disgust as Luke Soywalker tries to shoo the Engawa away.

Luke looks to Zen and says, "I can't understand how we got by those saketroopers. I thought we were fried."

Zen smiles and replies, "The Rice can have a strong influence on the weak-minded. You will find it a powerful ally."

A curious Luke asks, "Do you really think we're going to find a spacefish pilot here that'll take us to Abaloneraan?"

"Well, most of the best spacefish freighter pilots can be found here.

Only watch your soy. This place can be a little rough."

A confident Luke replies, "I'm ready for anything."

Soy-3PO, following Luke, calls out to Miso-D2, "Come along!"

The last thing I saw as I walked out of the sushi bar door was Junichi-san getting hit in the back of the head by Hiroshi-san for putting the open soy sauce bottle with the broken cap and a container holding leftover miso soup into the refrigerator.

Hiroshi-san scolded him by shouting in english, "Open soy sauce and today's miso do not go in the refrigerator! Stop wasting valuable space! Throw soy and miso away! Fresh for tomorrow." Then he yelled something in Japanese. Junichi-san furiously bowed and removed the open soy sauce bottle and miso container. Hiroshi-san looked at a clipboard on the side of the refrigerator and called out to Junichi-san, "We need room for the unagi tomorrow. Lots of fresh eel coming." I now knew how to occupy my time on the subway ride home. The sushi was coming with me and eel was coming in to the bar. Perfect.

Luke Soywalker and his two soyd servants follow Zen Wasabi into the steam-filled CannedTuna. A small sign reading "Chakin's Oceanport CannedTuna" hangs above the entrance. The cold, murky tin is filled with a startling array of weird and exotic alien fish and vegetables at a long bar, that looks like a metal grate. At first, the sight is horrifying. Scaled, shelled, skinned, slimy, tentacled, mushy, and clawed creatures huddle over drinks. Zen moves to an empty spot at the bar near a group of repulsive sushi scad that look like they are spoiling. A huge, rough-looking yellowtail bartender named Warasa stops Luke and the roebots.

Bartender Warasa bellows, "We don't serve their kind here!"

Luke, still recovering from the shock of seeing so many outlandish sushi creatures, doesn't quite catch the bartender's drift.

Luke replies, "What?"

Warasa leans in toward Luke and says, "Your soyds. They'll have to wait outside. We don't want them here."

Luke looks at old Zen, who is busy talking to one of the galaxsea pirates. He notices several of the gruesome creatures along the bar are giving him a very unfriendly glare. Luke pats Soy-3PO on the cap. "Listen, why don't you wait out by the trayspeeder. We don't want any trouble." Soy-3PO agrees.

We left Moto Sushi and walked to the subway station. My mom inserted her transit card into the machine at the gate and it beeped intensely at her. Her card was rejected by the machine. She sighed heavily, led my father by the hand, and brought us over to the ticket counter to refill her card. The attendant was as rude as he was suppose to be, working in mass transit, dealing with the general public. Once her card was loaded, we resumed our journey home. My mind drifted back to Moto Sushi's refrigerator and the to-go containers I was carrying. And I thought of the eel to be delivered.

Soy-3PO and Miso-D2 go outside and most of the creatures at the bar go back to their drinks. Zen is standing next to Unagibacca, an eight-centimeter-tall, savage-looking creature, a Wookieel, resembling a slimy, huge brown-sauced eel with fierce fangs. His large black roe eyes dominate a sauce-covered face and soften his otherwise intimidating appearance. Over his slimy, saucy body he wears two rice bandoliers and little else. He is a two-hundred-minute-old Wookieel and a sight to behold. Zen speaks to the Wookieel, pointing to Luke several times during his conversation and the huge creature suddenly lets out a horrifying laugh. Luke is more than a little bit disconcerted and pretends to ignore the conversation between Zen and the giant Wookieel. Luke is terrifried but tries not to show it. He quietly sips his drink, looking over the crowd for a more sympathetic ear or whatever might calm him.

We loaded into the right subway train to ride home. I sat on an empty seat next to my mom and dad and placed the to-go containers side by side on the other seat next to me. I peered into the leftovers and then into the ones that Hiroshi-san gave us in case we got hungry on the ride home, which didn't matter to me. I'm not eating this stuff. The train jerked forward and the two containers banged into each other.

A large, seaweed wrapped veggie creature at the bar gives Luke a rough shove and utters "Negola dewaghi wooldugger?!?"
The hideous seaweed veggie creature is obviously drunk. Luke tries to ignore the creature and turns back on his drink. A short, grubby rainbow fish sushi, Ponda Bera, joins the belligerent monstrosity.
"He doesn't like you," threatens Ponda Bera.
Luke apologizes.
"I don't like you either," responds Ponda Bera.
The big seaweed veggie creature is getting agitated and yells out some unintelligible gibberish at the now rather nervous, young Soywalker.
Ponda Bera continues, "Don't insult us. You just watch yourself. We're wanted sushi. I have the fry sentence in twelve tidal zones."
Luke replies, "I'll be careful then."

Ponda quickly and loudly retorts, "You'll be eaten!"

The seaweed veggie creature grunts and everyone at the bar moves away. Luke tries to remain cool but it isn't easy. His adversaries ready their laserbean weapons. Old Zen moves in behind Luke and says, "This little one isn't worth the effort. Come let me buy you something…"

A powerful blow from Ponda Bera sends the young would-be Red-Eye sailing across the room, crashing through folded napkins and breaking a large jug filled with a foul-looking liquid. With a soy-curdling shriek, the sushi monster draws a wicked green laserbean pistol from his belt and levels it at old Zen. The bartender, Warasa, panics and screams, "No laserbeans! No laserbeans!" With astounding agility old Zen's chopsabers spark to life and in a flash a fin lies on the floor. Zen carefully and precisely turns off his chopsabers and replaces them onto his utility belt. Luke, shaking on the floor and totally amazed at the old wasabi's abilities, attempts to stand. The entire fight has lasted only a matter of seconds. The CannedTuna goes back to normal, although Zen is given a respectable amount of room at the bar. Luke, trying to unmush his mushed soy head, approaches the old wasabi with new awe.

Zen nods at the Wookieel. Zen says, "This is Unagibacca. He's first-bait on a spacefish that might suit our needs."

We got off the subway at our usual stop and made our way to our home. That was enough sushi adventure for one night. I must admit though, as I started drifting off to sleep that night, I thought about sushi and how all of those gross raw fish parts actually worked out well as characters in my Star… um, I mean, Sushi Wars adventure. I was actually looking forward to returning to Moto Sushi next Friday night. That was a first.

5 THE MILLENNIUM FLOUNDER

The following Friday was like any other Friday. I finished school, went home and watched some television and played my Star Wars video game again, trying to get through the Empire Strikes Back level. Still no luck. Seems like the Rebels had an easier time on Hoth than I did trying to get them off Hoth in the game! My father came home from work around six o'clock and we all headed to the subway to return to Moto Sushi as usual. The difference this time was that I was actually looking forward to getting back to the sushi restaurant. After all, I had an adventure to continue. The dreaded Mos Icely CannedTuna, the refrigerator, and all the mysterious and ominous creatures it held called to me. Of course, I would still order my usual kushi and fend off the persistent nagging of Hiroshi-san on telling me I needed to eat sushi not kushi. I still hated sushi, well, at least to eat. I just happened to have found a better use for it now.

We walked down the street and were just about to enter Moto Sushi when a tall, dark man in a black coat calmly but hurriedly exited out of the doors carrying a bottle of soy sauce and approached two policemen standing on the corner of the street. I looked up at my mom and she shrugged her shoulders. My father looked inside Moto Sushi and it was busy but there was no sign of trouble so he too shrugged his shoulders and we went inside. I looked back at the tall, dark man and saw him point at Moto Sushi as he was explaining something to the policemen. He pointed at the soy sauce bottle, then back to Moto Sushi. They exchanged a few words and gestures until the policemen looked a bit annoyed. The tall, dark man nodded with a frown in defeat. Whatever he was complaining about didn't warrant the policemen's attention.

Soy-3PO paces in front of the Mos Icely CannedTuna as Miso-D2 carries on a conversation with another little red hydro-soyd. An unidentifiable piece of sushi shrouded in seaweed exits the CannedTuna and approached two saketroopers in the alley between large shells.

Soy-3PO looked at Miso-D2 and uttered, "I don't like the look of this."

We entered Moto Sushi and, as usual, Hiroshi-san looked up from behind the bar said something that sounded like "I rash sim mass hay." I never understood what he said but for some reason I had the urge to bow a little. So, I bowed a little. Hiroshi-san pointed his knife toward our usual seating area at the end of the bar by the bamboo wall. I once asked my dad what Hiroshi-san says when we enter since he had been to Japan. He obviously didn't know but told me it was something like "fresh fish, come in, sit down over there." I go to school with a Japanese kid so maybe I'll ask him someday if I remember.

We sat down at our usual seats and Hiroshi-san immediately brought out a special white dish containing three pieces of unagi, freshly cooked eel on rice, and two slightly pinkish prawns with a small pile of fresh wasabi and one piece atsuage, deep-fried tofu. He placed the dish in front of my mom so we could all share.

Hiroshi-san, bowed and said, "Small gift to make sure friendship last long time. No charge. Unagi for all. Prawn for mom and dad and atsuage for the boy. Hmm? Good." He nodded his approval of our approval.

My mother placed her hands over her mouth as moms do when they act surprised as she let out an endearing "awww". My parents proudly accepted the offering and thanked Hiroshi-san for his thoughtfulness. My father again apologized for last week's starfish debacle. Junichi-san brought over the sushi checklists for their order, bowing profusely and hoping not to get hit in the head by Hiroshi-san after serving us. I quickly grabbed the plate of sushi offerings. How could this be? All of the essential items for the CannedTuna scenes. Score! I picked off the atsuage, a gob of wasabi, and one of the unagi pieces and placed them on my plate. My mother, eying the prawns, was a bit surprised that I took anything off the serving plate but was quickly distracted by my father's elbow jabbing her ribs to validate a story he had already started with the unsuspecting customer we sat next to. Poor chap. Poor mom. Some traditional Japanese music started playing over the speakers.

Strange sushi creatures play exotic big band music on odd-looking instruments as Luke, still giddy, downs a fresh drink and follows Zen and Unagibacca to a folded napkin where Prawn Solo is sitting. Prawn is a tough, rogue-like spacefish pilot about thirty hours old, an overcooked reddish-pink prawn, but certainly clammanding. A mercenary with a spacefish, he is simple, sentimental, cocky, and shellfish enough to only care about himself.

As my mom became distracted, I grabbed one of the prawns with my fingers and put it on my plate as well with no intention of ever eating it. She grabbed the checklist and started checking off their order for the night, consulting with my dad between forced laughs, unintelligible jokes and bloated short stories.

Prawn Solo eyes Zen Wasabi and says, "Prawn Solo. I'm captain of the Millennium Flounder. Unagi here tells me you're looking for passage to the Abaloneraan tidal zone."

Zen Wasabi responds, "Yes, indeed. If it's a fast spacefish."

Prawn looks surprised at the comment and says, "Fast spacefish? You've never heard of the Millennium Flounder?"

Zen replies, "Should I have?"

"It's the spacefish that made the Mussel Run in less than twelve nautical miles!"

Zen looks at Prawn with a heavy dose of doubt, not about the performance of the Millennium Flounder per se, but more about the fact that Prawn Solo just used a measurement of length to describe what should have been a measurement of time. He shrugs off the notion giving Prawn the benefit of the doubt, assuming he meant the Millennium Flounder was capable of escaping the strong pull of vortices in the Mussel Run tidal zone and therefore was able to find a shorter route through the treacherous waters, hence Prawn's use of distance versus time, but that could be debated forever and probably will be.

Prawn continues, "I've outrun Imperial spacefish, not the local bulky Stargazers, mind you. I'm talking about the big Corallian spacefish now. She's fast enough for you, old wasabi. What's the es-cargo?"

Zen Wasabi smiles and replies, "Only passengers. Myself, the soy, two soyds, and no questions asked."

Prawn smiles back and asks, "What is it? Some kind of local trouble? You water down a land solidifier or something?"

"Let's just say we'd like to avoid any Imperial entanglements. No nets."

"Well, that's the trick, isn't it? And it's going to cost you something extra. Ten thousand cowry shells in advance."

Luke chimes in after watching the conversation at this point and indignantly asks, "Ten thousand? We could almost buy our own spacefish for that!"

Prawn pokes back, "But who's going to swim it, kid? You?"

Prawn snickers.

Luke's ego speaks for him, "You bet I could! I'm not such a bad pilot myself! We don't have to sit here and listen…"

Zen interrupts, "We haven't that much with us. But we could pay you two thousand now, plus fifteen when we reach Abaloneraan."

Prawn calculates using his periopods, his pleopods, and even his uropods. He eventually nods satisfied that his high level math is correct and says, "Seventeen, huh?" He ponders this for a moment, rethinking his math a bit but nods again to himself as he lowers all of his pods.

"Okay, you guys got yourself a spacefish. We'll leave as soon as you're ready. Docking Bay Ninety-Four."

Zen echoes back, "Ninety-Four."

Prawn gazes beyond Zen Wasabi and sees some saketroopers talking with the bartender and informs Zen, "Looks like somebody's beginning to take an interest in your finwork."

Zen and Luke turn around to see four Imperial saketroopers looking around and asking the bartender some questions. The bartender points to the folded napkin where they are sitting.

The saketroopers look over at the napkin but Luke and Zen are gone. Warasa, the bartender, shrugs in puzzlement.

Prawn looks at Unagibacca and says, "Seventeen thousand cowry shells! Those guys must really be desperate. This could really save my shell. Get back to the spacefish and get her ready."

Back in the shell alley, on the side of the Mos Icely CannedTuna, Zen tells Luke, "You'll have to sell your trayspeeder."

A determined Luke replies, "That's okay. I'm never coming back to this plate again."

My mother called over Hiroshi-san and asked for his recommendation on some vegetables to accommodate their selections of sushi. Hiroshi-san looked over his glasses and scanned her checklist. He thought for a second.

Hiroshi-san then said, "Ah, edamame, of course, and maybe fresh burdock root... from Japan just yesterday... with some nice, locally grown carrots sliced thin for kinpira gobo dish. Really nice. I braise with soy sauce, some sugar, sake, and sesame oil."

My mother looked impressed and replied, "That would be very nice, Hiroshi-san. Thank you."

They discussed other aspects of the order for a little while. Minutes later, some edamame and the kinpira gobo dish arrived at our section of the bar courtesy of Junichi-san, ahead of the rest of the order. It was a nice looking dish. Carrots and burdock root chopped julienne style, braised in the soy-based sauce in an oddly-shaped white dish with a raised lip on one side. I grabbed a bunch of the burdock root with my chopsticks and lined them up on my plate next to the prawn.

Inside the CannedTuna, Prawn Solo is about to leave when Gobo, a slimy root-faced creature with a short stick-like nose, pokes a laserbean blaster in Prawn's side. The root creature speaks in a foreign tongue but Prawn Solo seems to understand.

Gobo, in his native tongue, says, "Going somewhere, Solo?"

Prawn Solo calmly responds, "Not solo. Unagibacca is with me. Duh."

Gobo sighed, rolled his alien eyes and began to look impatient.

Prawn continued, "Well, yes, okay Gobo. As a matter of fact, I was just going to see your boss. Tell Wasaba that I've got his cowry shells."

Prawn sits down at the folded napkin and Gobo sits across from him holding the laserbean blaster on him.

Gobo says, "It's too late. You should have paid him when you had the chance. Wasaba's put a price on your carapace so large that every bounty hunter in the oceanverse will be looking for you. I'm lucky I found you first."

Prawn calmly responds, "Yeah, but this time I got the cowry shells."

Gobo considers the situation and offers, "If you give it to me, I might forget I found you."

Prawn replies, "I don't have it with me. Tell Wasaba…"

Gobo interrupts, "Wasaba's through with you. He has no time for pink smugglers who drop their shipments at the first sign of an Imperial spacefish."

"Even I get a lamprey sometimes. Do you think I had a choice?" Prawn Solo slowly reaches for his laserbean blaster under the napkin. Gobo continues, "You can tell that to Wasaba. He may only take your spacefish."

"Over my fried body!"

"That's the idea. I've been looking forward to frying you for a long time," replies a satisfied Gobo.

Prawn says, "Yes, I'll bet you have."

I spread out the individual burdock root slices and popped out the beans of an edamame pod at the root slices. I took a small bite out of a few of the root strands and dropped the remnants on and around the plate unceremoniously. I smiled, less about the taste and more about the scattered remnants. A few of the edamame beans scattered around my plate. My mother scolded me, already, by straining my name under her breath with a look of fury on her face.

I showed my teeth in a fake smile filled with apology and said, "Sorry about the mess, mom."

Suddenly the slimy root creature is immersed in a blinding green flash of edamame beans. His root slices separate almost instantly and fall to the floor in pieces, some emitting steam. Prawn pulls his steaming laserbean blaster from beneath the napkin as the other patrons look on in bemused amazement. Prawn gets up and starts out of the CannedTuna, flipping Warasa, the bartender, some cowry shells as he leaves.

Prawn looks right at Warasa, and says, "Sorry about the mess. He was the root of all evil."

Junichi-san knew my parents would order sake as they do every Friday night, so as if on cue, he brought 2 small 300 milliliter bottles over to my father with 2 sake cups and placed them by their empty miso soup bowls. My mother usually only had one cup of sake but my father would toast any one who would listen to the toasts he made. And once they accepted one, it was difficult for them not to accept a second and so was how the nights at the sushi bar usually went. Junichi-san brought me a glass of water as usual. Hiroshi-san then came over to fill each of our miso bowls with steaming hot miso soup.

Two heavily-finned saketroopers move menacingly along a narrow, slimy seaweed alley crowded with darkly clad sushi creatures hawking exotic goods in the moldy little stalls. Sushi, sashimi, and roebots crouch in the waste-filled poreways, whispering and hiding from the strong tides.

Soy-3PO, hiding in one of the stalls, ask Miso-D2 to lock the pore. One of the saketroopers checks a tightly locked pore and moves on down the seaweed alley. The pore slides open a crack and Soy-3PO peeks out. Miso-D2 is barely visible behind Soy-3PO. The saketroopers check the other side of the seaweed alley and find nothing. They move further away down the seaweed alley. Soy-3PO doesn't understand what the trouble is all about but is sure it is Miso-D2's fault and tells him so. Miso-D2 burps at Soy-3PO, who stands shocked at Miso-D2's harsh language.

As Hiroshi-san and Junichi-san work on my parents' sushi order, I call out to Hiroshi-san and ask if I can have the same kushi dinner I had last week.

He refused to look up at me but answered me, "No sushi again Billy-san? Kushi not as good as sushi but I will make for you if I must. Maybe slightly different, but still kushi, ok?"

I nodded, forcing him to look up at me when he didn't hear an immediate response from me. He looked at me and gave a fake smile as he looked back at his work.

The tall, dark man that left Moto Sushi as we were coming in, reentered with a stern look on his face. I still didn't know why he left the restaurant with a bottle of soy sauce and went to talk to the police officers. He looked around the restaurant as if he was looking for someone or something. Junichi-san stopped what he was doing behind the bar to watch the tall, dark man. He walked across the restaurant, returned the bottle of soy sauce to his table and sat down. Hiroshi-san gazed over his glasses as the tall, dark man sat down at the table in the back of the restaurant facing the sushi bar and then calmly resumed his full attention to the preparation of someone's sushi order as he sucked his teeth. Something was odd about this tall, dark man and I thought Hiroshi-san and Junichi-san knew something about what was going on with him.

There was a couple sitting at the table next to the tall, dark man just finishing their dinner. Their check was on the table. As the woman finished her drink, her husband placed some money on the check tray and stacked a bunch of coins on the table, presumably for a tip. They got up and left the restaurant, nodding thanks to Hiroshi-san as they left and seemed anxious to leave.

Zen Wasabi and Luke Soywalker are standing on a sleazy, mossy back dock area, talking with a tall, grotesque water strider insect employed as a used trayspeeder dealer. Strange slug-like creatures pass by as the water strider dealer concludes the sale by giving Luke some cowry shells as payment.

Luke approaches Zen and says, "He says it's the best he can do. Since the XP-38 came out, they're just not in demand."

Zen comforts Luke and says it'll be enough.

Zen and Luke leave the trayspeeder dock and slide down the damp shell alley past a small roebot herding a bunch of seahorse-like creatures. Luke turns and gives one last forlorn look at his faithful trayspeeder as he rounds a corner. A darkly clad seaweed creature moves out of the shadows as they pass and watches them as they disappear down another alley.

Zen further comforts Luke by stating, "If the spacefish is as fast as he's boasting, we ought to do well."

My dad started telling the neighboring patron at the sushi bar about the time he visited a wasabi root farm in Japan. The fellow patron responded with many nods suggesting he knew what my dad was talking about. My father then started exaggerating as he was prone to do when someone seemed interested in his stories. He talked about how he plucked a wasabi root and gnawed at it with his teeth to see what kind of real flavor there was in the root. The neighbor seemed confused at this. My dad back-pedaled a little and said well he scraped it with his fingernail and tasted it that way.

My mother was looking at my father with a look that demanded his honesty. She raised an eyebrow and called over to Junichi-san. Junichi-san came quickly over. My mother asked her for a wasabi root, not the paste, but just the root so they could see if my dad could indeed taste it by scraping his fingernail over it. She asked using a lot of grating motions with her hands to ensure Junichi-san understood what she wanted. He bowed. This request made my dad notice her skepticism about his story and he sighed at her with obvious nervous displeasure. The neighboring customer smiled.

Junichi-san approached our section of the sushi bar and bowed heavily as he placed a shark-skin covered wasabi grating board in front of my mom. On the board sat a very large piece of raw wasabi root and some recently grated wasabi. Junichi-san also brought over a small dish of special soy sauce, some pickled ginger root, and purple radish on a small plate.

Junichi-san addressed my mom, "Wasabi root for josei. No eat this way! Ok? Ok."

My mom bowed in thanks. She seemed pleased to now be able to prove my father an embellisher. My dad ignored this now as he told our neighboring patron all about his most recent trip to Japan which did not include a visit to a wasabi farm. I realized there was no way I was going to be able to steal the wasabi root, especially one so large. So, I waddled my prawn over to the edge of the shark-skin board. My mom looked at me with a puzzled look at first and then turned her attention to bring my dad back to the wasabi-fingernail dispute. He wasn't about to comply and started back-pedaling on his story again. This gave me just enough time to play a bit.

I also finished eating the burdock root to remove any evidence of the shooting of edamame incident. It wasn't all that bad to the taste and, more importantly, it contained no raw fish.

Wasaba the Root, a half-dozen pickled gari pirates and some purple radish creatures stand in the middle of Docking Bay Ninety-Four. Wasaba is the grossest mass of any slavering root and his scarred face is a grim testimonial to his ability to survive as a vicious killer. He is a fat, knot-covered piece of wasabi root with large, pale eyes and a huge gaping slice for a mouth.

Wasaba calls out for Prawn Solo, "Come on out, Prawn Solo!"

A voice from directly behind the pickled gari pirates startles them. They turn around to see Prawn Solo and the giant Wookieel, Unagibacca, standing behind them with no weapons in sight.

Prawn replies, "I've been waiting for you, Wasaba."

"I expected you would be."

Prawn retorts, "I'm not the type to swim away."

Wasaba says, "Prawn, my shrimp, there are times when you disappoint me...why haven't you paid me? And why did you have to fry poor Gobo like that...after all we've been through together."

"You sent Gobo to deep fry me."

In mock surprise, Wasaba responds, "Prawn, why you're the best fish smuggler in the business. You're too valuable to fry. He was only relaying my concern at your delays. He wasn't going to deep fry you."

"I think he thought he was. Next time don't send one of those veggie-twerps. If you've got something to say to me, come see me yourself."

"Prawn, Prawn! If only you hadn't had to dump that shipment of ocha...you understand I just can't make an exception. Where would I be if every pilot who smuggled for me dumped their shipment at the first sign of an Imperial spacefish? It's not good business."

"You know, even I get a lamprey sometimes, Wasaba. I had no choice, but I've got a charter now and I can pay you back, plus a little extra. I just need some more time."

Wasaba the Root addresses his crew of pirates and creatures, "Put your laserbean blasters away."

"Prawn, my shrimp, I'm only doing this because you're the best and I need you. So, for an extra, say twenty percent, I'll give you a little more time...but this is it. If you disappoint me again, I'll put a price on your carapace so large you won't be able to go near a civilized tidal zone for the rest of your short shell life.

Prawn Solo smiles and replies, "Wasaba, I'll pay you because it's my pleasure."

I pulled the prawn away from the wasabi grater board just as my mom went to grab the root to have my dad prove he could sample a taste from scraping it with his fingernails. She was going to enjoy see him writhe a little bit in hopes he wouldn't exaggerate so much next time.

The tall, dark man in the back of the restaurant got up from his seat and headed past me and went into the restroom. Just as he was about to enter the restroom, he pulled a small flip notebook and a pen from his shirt pocket. His eyes darted into the restroom before he entered. He stiffened his jaw and went inside. The door closed and locked behind him. Hiroshi-san was too busy to notice, but did notice that the table where the man sat was now empty. He glanced around the room but did not see him anywhere or anything out of the ordinary. He began to look just a little nervous.

Unagibacca waits restlessly at the entrance to Docking Bay Ninety-Four. Zen, Luke, and the roebots make their way up the street. Unagibacca jabbers excitedly and signals for them to hurry. The darkly clad seaweed creature has followed them from the trayspeeder lot and stops in a nearby poreway to speak into a small transfinner.

Junichi-san arrived with the first dish for my father, a couple of large flounder sushi pieces, known as karei, arranged on a bamboo serving tray, each sitting on a flat bed of seaweed. One of the larger pieces was browning a bit. My father eyed the dish over and frowned when he saw the browned piece. He called over Hiroshi-san after dismissing Junichi-san with a nod, a slight bow and a fake smile. This put an end to my mom's ploy to call him out on the wasabi root. My dad looked very disappointed and concerned all of sudden.

Unagibacca leads the group into a giant swampy shell indentation that is Docking Bay Ninety-Four. Resting in the middle of the huge moldy hole is a large, round, bruised, flat flounder that could only loosely be called a spacefish.

Luke comments, "What a piece of fluke."

Prawn Solo comes down the boarding ramp of the Millennium Flounder.

Prawn replies, "She'll make point five beyond the speed of riptide. She may not look like much, but she's got it where it counts, soy. I've added some special floundifications myself."

Luke squints at the Millennium Flounder and is clearly not too sure about any of this. Unagibacca rushes up the ramp and urges the others to follow.

Prawn urges, "We're a little rushed, so if you'll hurry aboard we'll get out of here."

The group rushes up the gang plank into the Millennium Flounder past a sarcastically grinning Prawn Solo. As Soy-3PO waddles past Prawn, he greets him quite formally. Prawn rolls his black roe eyes.

Hiroshi-san came over to tend to my father. He pointed to the browning flounder sushi and asked Hiroshi-san if he had anything fresher. Hiroshi-san looked down at the browning karei. His eyes grew large, looked out the corner of his eyes to either side.

He bowed at my father, very embarrassed and said, "So sorry. Oxidation cause browning, not unfresh fish. Hmm. I replace right away.

Sorry. So sorry."

My mom looked a little disappointed and realized that the moment with the wasabi root had passed. She realized that if she made fun of him now, it would appear spiteful. She was fine with a little embarrassment but the browned sushi piece of flounder certainly altered the mood at the bar.

Inside the Millennium Flounder, Unagibacca settles into the pilot's seat and starts the mighty gills of the spacefish.

Hiroshi-san took the entire tray back behind the bar, looked above his glasses, scanning the room. He looked precisely at the table where the tall, dark man was originally sitting and seemed concerned that he was not there. He placed the browned flounder sushi onto the bar counter and placed a fresh piece of flounder sushi that showed no signs of browning onto the serving tray.

He returned the tray to my father and said, "No problem. This dish is on the house tonight. Very sorry."

My father seemed very pleased with this offer and replied, "No issue, Hiroshi-san. Thank you." He then quickly resumed his story with the neighboring patron who was actually now enjoying my dad's stories. Out came the sake. My mom replaced the wasabi root onto the grater.

Hiroshi-san went over to Junichi-san and whispered something to him, pointing at the refrigerator in the back of the bar. Junichi-san bowed and nodded as he shuffled over to the refrigerator. He open the large door and started inspecting the temperature controls. They were not where they should have been. He adjusted a knob or two and then inspected the contents, nodding as each dish passed inspection.

The tall, dark man returned from the restroom looking over the bar. At the same time, Junichi-san, as if sensing danger behind him, quickly closed the refrigerator door and stiffly shuffled away ensuring not to look across the bar at all. I looked at the tall, dark man, and saw him pause for a moment while looking at Junichi-san. He peered over the bar counter, saw the browning flounder sushi, raised one eyebrow, smirked, glanced at the refrigerator, and then returned to his seat without saying a word. Once he sat down, he made some notes in his small notebook.

My mom waved over Junichi-san as she thought he was looking at her but really he was actually looking around her at the tall, dark man. He noticed her waving and came over. She motioned that she was done with the wasabi root and the shark-skin grating board. He took it away.

Just seconds later, the back door delivery bell rang, which was unusual. Moto Sushi usually did not accept deliveries during the dinner rush. Junichi-san shuffled to the back door and let in a man pushing around two boxes with a hand truck. Hiroshi-san waved him in behind the edge of the bar. The delivery man placed two cases of sake on the floor behind the bar, right in front of us. They clanked against one another as they settled on the floor.

Back near the entrance of Docking Bay Ninety-Four, eight Imperial saketroopers roll up to the darkly clad seaweed creature.

The lead saketrooper asked the creature, "Which way?"

The dark creature points to the pore of the docking bay.

"All right, bottles. Load your weapons!"

The saketroopers hold their laserbean blasters at the ready and charge down the docking bay entrance.

The lead saketrooper yells out, "Stop that spacefish!"

Prawn Solo looks up and sees the Imperial saketroopers rushing into the moldy docking bay. Several of the saketroopers fire at Prawn as he ducks into the spacefish.

"Blast 'em," cries a nearby saketrooper.

Prawn draws his laserbean pistol and pops off a couple of bean shots which force the saketroopers to topple and clank to the floor for safety. The spacefish gills whine as Prawn hits the release button that slams the overhead entry shut.

Prawn yells up the main corridor of the Millennium Flounder, "Unagi, get us out of here!"

The group hurriedly straps in for take off.

Soy-3PO complains, "Oh, my. I'd forgotten how much I hate oceanverse travel."

Hiroshi-san bowed to the delivery man as he left through the back door. The door chimed as the man exited. Hiroshi-san then saw the browning flounder sushi still sitting on the counter top. He called out to Junichi-san in Japanese, nodding at the browning flounder sushi as he was preparing another sushi specialty. Junichi-san quickly shuffled over to the oxidized flounder and tossed it into the air over the sake cases into the trash can. I watched the flounder fly through the air and disappear into the black liner of the trash can. Junichi-san looked at me nervously. I simply shook my head from side to side. He frowned and disappeared into the kitchen.

A group of saketroopers at a nearby checkpoint hear the general alarm and look up to the sky as the huge spacefish rises above the moldy slum dwellings and quickly disappears into the morning sky.

Prawn Solo climbs into the pilot's chair next to Unagibacca, who chatters away as he points to something on the sonar scope. The Corallian pirate spacefish, known as the Millennium Flounder, zooms from Tidetooine into the open oceanverse. Prawn frantically types information into the spacefish's brain. Miso-D2 appears momentarily at the fishhead poreway, makes a few burping remarks, and then scurries away.

Prawn informs the group, "It looks like an Imperial Stargazer. Our passengers must be hotter than I thought. Try and hold them off. Angle the deflector fin while I make the calculations for the jump to riptide speed."

Junichi-san grabbed two large, dirty, wooden serving trays from the counter top and brought them over to the trash can. He scraped the food remnants off the trays into the trash can with a large rubber spatula. The food remnants fall into void of the trash can.

The Millennium Flounder spacefish races away from the oceanic plate, Tidetooine. It is followed by two huge Imperial Stargazers. Before Unagibacca and Prawn lies the open spread of the galaxsea. Luke and Zen make their way into the cramped fishhead where Prawn pilots the spacefish and continues his calculations.

Prawn yells out, "Stay sharp! There are two more coming in. They're going to try to fillet us."

Luke replies, "Why don't you outswim them? I thought you said this thing was fast."

"Watch your mouth, soy, or you're going to find yourself floating home, belly up. We'll be safe enough once we make the jump to hypersea. Besides, I know a few fineuvers. We'll lose them!"

The Imperial Stargazers fire laserbeans at the Millennium Flounder. The Millennium Flounder shudders as a bean explosion flashes outside the fishhead eyes.

"Here is where the fun begins," exclaims Prawn.

Zen asks, "How long before you can make the jump to riptide speed?"

"It'll take a few moments to get the menu of coordinates from the navi-brain."

The Millennium Flounder begins to rock violently as the laserbeans hit it.

Luke butts in, "Are you kidding? At the rate they're gaining…"

Prawn interrupts, "Traveling through hypersea isn't like misting seaweed on Tidetooine, soy! Without precise calculations we could swim right through a plate or bounce too close to a super tide, a tsunami, and that'd end your trip real quick, wouldn't it?"

The Millennium Flounder is constantly battered with laserbeans as red warning pulses begin to flash in the fishhead veins.

Luke, panicking, asks, "What's that flashing?"

A stressed Prawn responds, "We're losing our deflector fin. Go strap yourself in, I'm going to make the jump to riptide speed."

The galaxsea brightens and they move faster, almost as if crashing through a barrier. Plates become streaks as the spacefish makes the jump to hypersea. The Millennium Flounder zooms into in-fin-ity in less than a second.

Junichi-san cleared some of the dishes including what was left of the pickled gari, the purple radishes, and the kinpira gobo. The missing pieces were eaten by my mother.

6 THE TRACTOR BEAN

As Junichi-san finished scraping the wooden trays clean, I asked him about the garnishes around the unagi. I had never really known what these berry-looking things were. I needed to know because they oddly looked a lot like the training droids used when Luke first used his lightsaber in the first movie. They could be little floating balls of power ready to zap any Red-Eye trainee. Junichi-san had a hard time understanding that I even wanted his attention much less that I wanted to have a conversation with him. I asked him, in a normal tone, what the berries were called. He became very confused with the word 'berries'. So, after pointing to the berries with my chopsticks and shrugging my shoulders saying, "What are they?", I realized I might actually get an answer.

He said, "Ah. Bellies? Uh... sorry, be..err..ies... berries. We call sansho. Sansho... is uh... peppel. Uh... pep... pep. No... ah...pepp-errr. Yah. Pepperrrr." He emphasized his letter 'r' in every word to try and improve his english. I know Hiroshi-san has been on him about learning english better. He actually did surprisingly well this time.

"Ok, sansho, like pepper," I replied nodding. He returned to his work shaking his head ever so subtlety, mouthing the 'Rrrrr' sound.

Inside the Millennium Flounder, Zen Wasabi watches Luke Soywalker practice using the chopsabers with a small sansho training roebot. The sansho moves about erratically in the vicinity of Luke, circling him, spicing him whenever his guard is down or he becomes distracted.

Zen suddenly turns away and sits down. He falters and seems almost faint as he distantly stares through the bones of the Flounder.

Luke asks, "Are you all right? What's wrong?"

"I felt a great disturbance in the Rice... as if millions of sushiforms cried out in terror and were suddenly fried to silence. I fear something terrible has happened."

Zen Wasabi rubs his green head, sensing the mass frying of Abaloneraan as witnessed by Princess Maki, at the tentacles of Squid Vader and his Imperial forces. Zen seems to drift into a trance and then fixes his gaze on Luke.

He speaks to Luke, "You'd better get on with your exercises."

Prawn Solo enters the room and boasts, "Well, you can forget your troubles with those Imperial slugs. I told you I'd outswim 'em."

Luke continues to practice with his chopsabers in defeating the sansho.

Prawn surveys the room and sarcastically comments, "Don't everyone thank me at once. Not even a high fin, huh?"

My father continued his stories about Japan with the neighboring sushi bar customer. He talked about the time he was taught how to play Shogi, a version of Japanese chess. The neighboring customer nodded his headed vigorously and was apparently a very large fan of this game. My mother shook her head side to side and muttered, "Well, that did it," under her breath. She knew at that point that the night before her would be a long one. My father tempted his prey with curiosities, stories, and familiarity and when someone took the bait, they were locked in conversation for longer than they really wanted. I moved the miso bowl and the soy sauce bottle closer to the unagi on my plate.

Soy-3PO watches Unagibacca and Miso-D2 who are engrossed in a game in which three-dimensional rollographic figures move along a chessboard-type membrane.

Prawn continues, "Anyway, we should be at Abaloneraan about oh-two-hundred minutes."

Unagibacca and the two soyds sit around the lighted membrane covered with small rollographic seamonsters. Each side of the membrane has a small nerve cell embedded in it. Unagibacca seems very pleased with himself as he leans his lanky Wookieel body back in a proud and comfortable position.

My father continued his story about his first time playing Shogi and described how he was actually winning but saw that his Japanese host was getting very irritated. They discussed things like beginner's luck and how beginners don't know the traditions of strategy and therefore become unpredictable. My father then continued to tell the story and said he threw the game to ensure that his host won in order to preserve his host's reputation. He then said, "You know, it is important that the Japanese have a solid rep...," and then stopped as he quickly realized that he was speaking to a Japanese-American and most likely insulted him. So he continued, "But we Americans are rather boorish and not very sensitive to these things, am I right?"

My father felt his sushi bar companion losing interest as a frown emerged on his companion's face. He was slipping away. As usual, he nudged my mom in the ribs to contribute to the conversation to rescue him as he poured another small cup of sake for his newly insulted friend.

She obliged, resuscitated the conversation, and let out a heavy sigh after they resumed a cordial discussion. She was used to making excuses and apologies for my dad. It didn't even really phase her and it was a natural reaction to her ribs getting poked.

Soy-3PO warns Miso-D2 to be careful in the game as Miso-D2 immediately reaches up and taps the nerve cell surface with his stubby spoon, causing one of the rollographic sea creatures to swim to the new square. A sudden frown crosses Unagibacca's face and he begins yelling gibberish at the tiny roebot. Soy-3PO intercedes on behalf of his small companion and begins to argue with the huge Wookieel, "He made a fair move. Screaming about it won't help you."

Prawn Solo interrupts, "Let him have it. It's not wise to upset a Wookieel."

Soy-3PO replies, "But sir, nobody worries about upsetting a soyd."

Prawn smiles. "That's 'cause soyds don't pull sushi's rice out from under them when they lose. Wookieels are known to do that."

"I see your point, sir. I suggest a new strategy, Miso-D2. Let the Wookieel win."

Luke stands in the middle of the small hold area and seems frozen in place. He holds humming chopsabers high over his head. Zen watches him from the corner, studying his movements. Prawn watches with a bit of smugness.

Zen teaches, "Remember, a Red-Eye can feel the Rice flowing through him."

Luke asks, "You mean it controls your actions?"

Zen responds, "Partially. But it also obeys your clammands."

I tried to grab some of the berries, the sansho pepper, that came with the unagi with my chopsticks but I could not pick them up. I tried again and failed. Junichi-san saw this and started giggling.

Hiroshi-san came over, smiled at me, and said "Stretch out... with your fingers."

I smiled back as he continued into the kitchen behind the noren curtains. I stretched my fingers out a bit along the chopsticks and actually was able to pick up one of the sansho peppers. Junichi-san glanced at me, muttered something under his breath and probably thought it was just luck that I was able to pick up the sansho. He then went to the other side of the restaurant to clean up the tables after a large party that had just left.

Suspended at roe level, about ten millimeters in front of Luke, a sansho soyd, a reddish-brown ball-like roebot covered with antennae, hovers slowly in a wide arc. The sansho floats to one side of the youth then the other. Suddenly it makes a lightning-swift lunge and stops within a few feet of Luke's face. Luke doesn't move and the sansho backs off. It slowly moves behind the soy, then makes another quick lunge, this time spicing him as it attacks. It hits Luke in the lower crust causing him to tumble over. Prawn Solo lets loose with a burst of laughter as Luke inspects the pepper burn.

Prawn quips, "Hokey starches and ancient weapons are no match for a good laserbean blaster at your side, soy."

Luke sarcastically asks, "You don't believe in the Rice, do you?"

"Soy, I've swum from one side of this galaxsea to the other. I've seen a lot of strange stuff, but I've never seen anything to make me believe there's one all-powerful Rice controlling everything. There's no mystical rice field that controls my destiny."

Zen quietly smiles.

Prawn continues, "It's a lot of simple tricks and nonsense."

Zen addresses Luke. "I suggest you try it again, Luke."

My mother called over to Hiroshi-san and asked him for some green tea. He immediately nodded and moments later, Junichi-san brought over a small pot of tea and three chawans, Japanese tea bowls.

Zen places a large chawan, a tea bowl, on Luke's head which covers his red roe-eyes.

Zen instructs Luke, "This time, let go your conscious self and act on instinct."

Luke laughs and responds, "With the chawan lip pulled down, I can't even see. How am I suppose to fight?"

"Your roe-eyes can deceive you. Don't trust them."

Prawn skeptically shakes his head as Zen throws the sansho into the air. The sansho shoots straight up in the air, then drops like a rock.

Luke swings the chopsabers around blindly missing the sansho, which spices Luke square on the backside. He lets out a painful yell and attempts to hit the sansho.

Zen encourages, "Stretch out with your feelings."

Luke stands in one place, seemingly frozen. The sansho makes a dive at Luke and, incredibly, he manages to deflect the spice attempt. The sansho ceases fire and moves back to its original position.

Zen comments, "You see, you can do it."

Prawn smirks in disbelief, "I call it luck."

Zen replies, "In my experience, there's no such thing as luck."

Prawn says, "Look, going good against remote soyds is one thing. Going good against the raw? That's something else."

Prawn Solo notices a small pulse flashing on the far side of the control veins of the Millennium Flounder.

Our neighboring customer at the sushi bar interrupted my father's story as politely as possible and called over Hiroshi-san to order some food. Hirsohi-san hurriedly came over to him with a pencil and pad of paper. The customer ordered something in Japanese. As Hiroshi-san wrote down the order, he looked over at the tall, dark man at the back table splitting his attention between the tall, dark man and the Japanese customer speaking to him. The tall, dark man was staring directly at Hiroshi-san with a keen eye and Hiroshi-san shifted his entire focus to the tall, dark man. The Japanese customer felt a little ignored, like he wasn't even there and started looking behind him to see what had grabbed Hiroshi-san's attention.

I was confused as to what was going on with this tall, dark man. I wasn't even sure if Hiroshi-san knew him or not. They seemed to have some form of conflict going on but I was not sure what it was. I decided to look hard at the tall, dark man and try to discover some clues.

A shadow seemed to cover the tall, dark man wherever he went. He wore black clothes and a fedora with a front brim that hid his eyes well. He was indeed a relatively darker skinned man but not unusually so. He certainly was not Japanese. I saw him reach into his pocket once again and pull out the small notebook. As he did so, I spotted an all black tattoo of a starfish on each of his forearms. This left me further stumped. He obviously had a thing for sea creature tattoos but I still had no clue as to what he wanted or why Hiroshi-san was so concerned about his presence.

Hiroshi-san opened the ice box in front of him, instinctively thinking that whatever this customer was ordering would necessarily come out of this ice box in front of him. I had no idea what the customer was trying to order since it was in Japanese and at this point nothing was being said. I figured the customer was still upset about not having Hiroshi-san's full attention. He was getting a bit annoyed. This was very unlike Hiroshi-san. He was always very attentive to his customers. There was something very odd about this tall, dark man that really affected Hiroshi-san. As I pondered this, Hiroshi-san prepared some simple sea bass sushi for the neighboring patron. He obviously heard his order even if he hadn't quite acknowledged it.

Prawn informs everyone, "Looks like we're coming up on Abaloneraan."

Prawn Solo and Unagibacca head back to the fishhead.

Luke talks to Zen, "You know, I did feel something. I could almost see the remote soyd, the sancho."

Zen replies, "That's good. You have taken your first swim into a larger ocean."

Meanwhile, back on the Death Starfish, in a darkly decorated conference organ, Imperial Officer Bass stands before Governor Tarako and the evil Dark Lord Squid Vader.

Grand Moff Tarako acknowledges Imperial Officer Bass, "Yes?"

Officer Bass explains, "Our scout spacefish have reached Pantooine. They found the remains of a Rebel secret plate, but they estimate that is has been deserted for some time. They are now conducting an extensive search of the surrounding tidal zones."

Tarako becomes very mad and shouts out, "She lied! She lied to us!"

Squid Vader replies, "I told you she would never consciously betray the Rebellion."

In full rage, Tarako orders, "Fry her... immediately!"

The Millennium Flounder just comes out of hypersea and a strange surreal light show surrounds the spacefish.

Prawn Solo clammands the ship by instructing Unagibacca, "Stand by, Unagi. Here we go. Cut in the sub-riptide gills."

Junichi-san came back to the cabinets behind the bar after cleaning up many tables in the back of the restaurant and placed about 20 soy sauce dishes and roughly the same amount of chopsticks onto the back bar. He loaded his hands with the 20 or so soy sauce dishes and quickly shuffled over to the now clean tables. As he cruised by, he knocked into Hiroshi-san, who was still focused on the tall, dark man and in front of the customer feeling ignored, holding his order in his hands. This small bump shifted the balance of the soy sauce dishes in his small hands just enough to lose one onto the floor. In his attempt to catch that one soy sauce dish, he lost his balance and all of the soy sauce dishes flew out of his hands and plopped onto a very large flounder sitting on ice in the open bar ice box. Some clanked onto the bar, some plowed into the ice, some bopped off the flounder, and some bounced onto the floor. The fresh flounder seemed no worse for the wear.

Right at the moment of the incident, Hiroshi-san lowered his head as if something was about to fall on him. He spun around looking in the opposite direction of the tall, dark man and gazed at Junichi-san with a seriously mean and stressed look, but he said nothing. The customer whose order he held in his hands, let out an "ahem" in the most polite manner he felt he could muster. Junichi-san scurried about the back of the bar picking up all of the dropped soy sauce dishes, sorting them between clean dishes and dirty dishes.

Hiroshi-san sucked his teeth, held his head down low, and tried to shrug it all off by shaking his shoulders in a relatively dramatic and somewhat coordinated way. He sighed heavily and resumed his focus on the customer, bowing an apologetic bow. He placed the sea bass in front of the customer and further apologized for the distractions. He didn't look at Junichi-san for fear of yelling at him at this point and creating an even bigger scene. Junichi-san went along and set the tables with whatever clean dishes were left in his hands. A stack of dirty ones sat at the back bar, some of them clearly cracked and broken.

Prawn pulls back on the nerve control levers. Outside the fishhead eyes, plates begin streaking past seem to decrease in speed and then stop altogether. Suddenly, the spacefish begins to shudder and violently shake about. Fragments of shiny and ornate plates and small soy sauce dishes begin to race toward them, battering the sides of the spacefish.

Prawn exclaims, "What the...? Aw, we've come out of hypersea into a fancy plate and dish shower. Some kind of dropped plate or dish collision. It's not on any of the navigation menus. We're getting shelled!"

The Wookieel flips off several nerve controls and seems very cool in the emergency situation. Luke makes his way into the bouncing fishhead and asks, "What's going on?"

Prawn responds puzzled, "Our position is correct, except... no Abaloneraan!"

A confused Luke asks, "What do you mean? Where is it?"

"That's what I'm trying to tell you, soy. It ain't there. It's been totally blown away."

"What? How?"

Zen Wasabi moves into the fishhead behind Luke as the spacefish begins to settle down.

He looks out the fishhead eyes and says, "Destroyed... by the Tempura!"

Prawn looks back at Zen and replies, "The entire spacefish fleet couldn't destroy that whole plate. It'd take a thousand spacefish with more bean power than I've..."

A signal starts pulsing on the brain nerve panel and a muffled alarm starts humming.

Minutes later, after Hiroshi-san had calmed down, he emerged from the kitchen with a very large bowl in the shape of a starfish filled with gai sakamushi, steamed clams served in a sake broth. He held the dish with a very clean dish towel in order not to burn his hand. Each arm of the starfish bowl held four or five clams with a concentration of hot sake broth in the center. Steam was enveloping the top of the dish and flowed around Hiroshi-san's torso as he quickly delivered the warm dish to my parents. He placed the dish in front of my father and turned the dish so the majority of the clams, half opened, faced him for inspection and presentation, with the fifth point of the starfish bowl pointing toward the sushi bar. My father smelled the steam, coughed a little, and smiled broadly. This was a dish he had always wanted to try but never remembered to order. My mother had remembered and ordered it for him earlier. He clearly hadn't realized that as he immediately dug into the clams and pulled the first shell apart. The clam inside clung to the inner surface of both of the half-shells, stretching it across until it finally gave way. He used the serving spoon on the side of the dish to splash a bit of the sake broth onto the clam. My mom smiled at my father with anticipation of thanks coming her way for remembering and ordering the gai sakamushi. No such luck. In fact, he temporarily ignored the neighboring customer and my mom as he immersed himself in the steam, muscling each clam away from its shells and dunked each into the sake broth before slurping it down.

My mom shrugged her shoulders and seemed content with the fact that my dad was happy with this dish. The neighboring patron nodded his approval of the dish as well. As soon as Hiroshi-san delivered the gai sakamushi, he nodded to the customer seated next to my dad and said something in Japanese. Hiroshi-san said, "karei sushi, hai", and went right to work on his preparations of two karei sushi, thinly sliced flounder over rice.

Prawn reads the brain membranes and says, "There's another spacefish coming in."

Luke says, "Maybe they know what happened."

Zen informs, "It's an Imperial fighter."

Unagibacca barks his concern. A huge explosion bursts outside the fishhead eyes, shaking the spacefish violently. A tiny, shelled Imperial Gai Fighter races past the fishhead eyes.

Luke yells out, "It followed us!"

Zen replies, "No. It's a half-shell short range fighter."

Prawn becomes a bit scattered and reads multiple brain control membranes and nerve cells as he informs everyone that there are no secret plates around Abaloneraan's section. No one knows where the Gai Fighter came from. The Gai Fighter races past the Corallian-made Millennium Flounder.

Luke watches the flight path of the Gai Fighter and mentions that it is leaving and in a hurry. He warns that if they identify them then they're in big trouble. Prawn asks Unagibacca to jam it's tidemissions. Zen comments that it is well out of range already. Prawn moves the accelerator forward on the Millennium Flounder and chases the Gai Fighter in an attempt to destroy it before it can communicate with other Imperial contacts. Tension mounts in the fishhead of the Millennium Flounder as they gain on the lone Gai Fighter. In the distance, one of the platters becomes brighter until it is obvious that the Gai Fighter spacefish is heading for it.

Zen looks at the scene before them over Unagibacca in the fishhead and comments, "A Gai Fighter that size couldn't get this deep into the oceanverse on its own." Luke theorizes that it might have gotten lost or been a part of a clamvoy or something. Prawn Solo is determined to ensure the Gai Fighter won't be around long enough to tell anyone of the Flounder's presence.

The Gai Fighter is losing ground to the larger spacefish as they race toward the distant platter. What the crew of the Millennium Flounder thought was a platter, suddenly becomes distinguished as a small saucer plate.

Luke sees the Gai Fighter and says, "Look at him. He's headed for that small saucer."

Prawn, determined, states, "I think I can get him before he gets there. He's almost in bean range."

As they get closer, that small saucer plate reveals itself as an unbelievably large and oddly shaped battle station, the Death Starfish. The crew gets a very bad feeling about this situation as they realize the platter that was a plate became an Imperial battle station of unfathomable size and shape.

A shocked Zen Wasabi states the now obvious, "That's no saucer! It's a battle station!"

Prawn thinks out loud, "It's too big to be a battle station."

Luke chimes in nervously, "I have a very bad feeling about this."

Zen Wasabi calls out, "Yeah, I think you're right. Full reverse! Unagi, lock in the auxiliary power!"

The spacefish shudders and the Gai Fighter accelerates away toward the gargantuan battle station.

Luke asks, "Why are we still moving toward it?"

Prawn reads the brain control membrane and responds, "We're caught in a tractor bean! It's pulling us in!"

Luke panics, "But there's gotta be something you can do!"

Prawn replies, "There's nothin' I can do about it, soy. I'm in full power. I'm going to have to shut down. But they're not going to get me without a fight!"

Zen Wasabi puts a glob of wasabi on Prawn's shell and tells him, "You can't win. But there are alternatives to fighting."

After slurping two clams down, my father turned to my mom and offered her some. She politely shrugged and smiled as she ate some of the edamame. He then turned to the neighboring customer and offered some to him. He politely declined but then seemed to waft some of the steam his way as he was doing so. At that moment, Hiroshi-san served the karei to the customer and placed it right next to the starfish serving tray. The customer tilted his head back and forth slowly and then in fairly good english, asked my father if he would want to perhaps trade some gai sakamushi for a piece of his karei since both looked very appetizing. My father loved flounder so he quickly agreed. He instantly perked up and most likely saw this as an opportunity to further extend their conversation. My mother took one clam off the starfish serving tray and started fiddling with it in a very dainty way as to not get her hands too messy.

As the battered spacefish is towed closer to the massive plate before them by a tractor bean, the immense size of the Death Starfish becomes staggering to the crew of the Millennium Flounder. Running along the center arms of the Death Starfish is a long band of docking ports into which the helpless spacefish is dragged.

My father grabbed one of the karei off the neighbor's plate with his chopsticks and quickly then realized he had no where to really put it. His own dish was covered in clam shells and bits and pieces. He raised it up to his mouth as if to simply just eat the whole thing in one bite but then decided it needed some sauce. He dipped the bottom part of the karei sushi into the sake broth in the center of the starfish serving tray. The rice originally stuck to the karei started falling off and he quickly fed himself the karei with his other hand trailing behind it in order to catch any rice bits that might fall off.

As this was going on, Junichi-san was unpacking the recently delivered sake bottles near the edge of the sushi bar and placing them in a neat orderly manner on the shelves behind the bar in a meticulous formation with all the labels facing exactly the same way, clinking the occasional bottle on the shelf or other bottle.

The Millennium Flounder is pulled past a docking port control room and huge laserbean turret cannons. Overhead, a message is heard that states, "Clear Bay twenty-three-seven. We are opening the rice field." The spacefish is pulled in through port pores of the Death Starfish, coming to rest in a huge area. Thirty saketroopers stand at attention in a central assembly area. At clammand of the gill officer on the dock, the saketroopers waddle to their posts. A line of saketroopers slide toward the spacefish in readiness to board it, while other saketroopers stand with their laserbean pistols ready to fire. The officer orders the outer pores to be closed.

Watching Junichi-san unpack the sake bottles reminded me of the tall, dark man carrying the soy bottle again. I peered behind me and saw the tall, dark man still sitting at the table he originally sat at with his hat brim covering his eyes. On his table sat a serving kettle and small cup of hot tea, a small side dish of roe and a somewhat large dish of what appeared to be squid, or ika, and shrimp tempura. His notebook and pen rested at the edge of the table, both open and ready to use. I got a chill on my back as I turned back to face the sushi bar. There was something not quite right about this man. He wasn't simply here to eat. He appeared to be eating at a very slow pace. I had not even noticed Junichi-san or Hiroshi-san serving him. Perhaps one of the waitresses served him his meal. They typically served the tables and Hiroshi-san and Junichi-san usually just focused on the sushi bar patrons.

In a conference organ in an area of importance on the Death Starfish, Grand Moff Tarako sits next to Squid Vader, Lord of the Surf. Tarako answers a conuslink buzz and learns that a spacefish freighter whose markings match those of a spacefish that blasted its way out of Mos Icely has been captured as it entered the remains of the Abaloneraan tidal zone.

Squid Vader supposes, "They must be trying to return the stolen menus to the princess. She may yet be of some use to us."

Squid Vader and a clammander approach the saketroopers in docking bay 2037 as an officer and several heavily finned saketroopers roll out of the Millennium Flounder. The officer approaches Squid Vader and informs him that there is no one on board. He reports that the spacefish log recorded that the crew abandoned the spacefish right after takeoff. He suggests this is a decoy and further informs Vader that all of the escape eggs have been jettisoned.

Squid Vader asks, "Did you find any soyds?"

The officer reports, "No, sir. If there were any on board, they must also have jettisoned."

Squid Vader replies, "Send the scanning crawfish on board. I want every part of this spacefish checked."

"Yes, sir!"

Squid Vader speaks, but under his own breath, "I sense something... a presence I haven't felt since..."

Squid Vader quickly turns from the spacefish and exits the docking bay. The officer carries out Squid Vader's clammands and sends in the scanning crawfish.

7 SAKETROOPERS

The tall, dark man finished his meal, arranged his dishes in a very orderly manner for easy clean up, and dabbed his chin with his towelette. He then simply sat at his table, watching Hiroshi-san's every move and occasionally made notes in his notebook with deliberate motion. It was then that I realized that the tall, dark man had never once actually smiled.

Hiroshi-san was preparing more sushi behind the bar but would glance at the tall, dark man nervously from time to time.

Junichi-san finished placing the sake bottles on the shelf behind the bar and continued to arrange the labels such they all faced out in the same manner.

My father and the neighboring sushi bar customer continued to share stories as my father enjoyed his gai sakamushi and the neighboring customer enjoyed his last piece of karei sushi. I placed my towelette over my dish, covering the prawn, atsuage, and my pile of wasabi still on my plate from the beginning of the meal.

A saketrooper waddles through the hallway of the Millennium Flounder heading for the exit. In a few moments, all is quiet. The muffled sounds of a distant saketrooper officer giving orders finally fade. Two secret panels within the Millennium Flounder suddenly pop up revealing Prawn Solo and Luke Soywalker. Zen Wasabi peers out from a third pocket in the floor.

Luke addresses Prawn nervously, "Soy, it's lucky you had these compartments."

Prawn replies, "I use them for smuggling endangered fish. I never thought I'd be smuggling myself in them. This is ridiculous. Even if I could take off, I'd never get past the tractor bean."

Zen chimes in, "Leave that to me!"

Prawn looks at Zen in disbelief as if he were looking at a clam trying to swim upstream, "Clam fool. I knew you were going to say that!"

Zen retorts, "Who's the more foolish? The fool or the fool who follows him?"

Prawn shakes his head, muttering to himself. Unagibacca growls in agreement. Luke looks on perplexed and doesn't really understand what Prawn and Zen are talking about.

I took the cap from the half-empty sake bottle sitting in front of my mom and waved it over the towelette on my dish and then, without thinking, flung it against the bamboo wall next to me. The cap ricocheted off the bamboo at a very awkward angle, flew back over my dish, skipped off the sushi bar surface, pinged the sake bottle and landed spinning by my mom's dish just as she took the last edamame out of the serving bowl to her right. I then took the towelette off of my dish and placed it to the side.

The tall, dark man hadn't moved as if in a trance. He sat there and simply observed.

Two Imperial crawfish carry a heavy bottle scancap and approach the spacefish, past the two saketroopers guarding either side of the Millennium Flounder's loading ramp. One saketrooper allows them on board and clammands that if the scancap picks up anything to alert them immediately. The crayfish acknowledge and proceed up the ramp with the scancap. Seconds later, a loud crashing sound emanates from the spacefish and is followed with a voice calling down to the saketrooper guards below.

Prawn Solo calls out to them, "Hey down there. Could you give us a fin with this?"

The saketroopers enter the spacefish and a quick round of laserbean fire is heard. In a very small clammand ampulla in the Death Starfish bay near the entrance of the Millennium Flounder, an Imperial gill officer looks out over the forward bay and notices the saketrooper guards are missing.

He speaks into the conuslink, "TX-4-1-2. Why aren't you at your post? TX-4-1-2, do you copy?"

A saketrooper comes down the ramp of the spacefish and tips his cap to the gill officer, waving his cap and shaking his bottleneck back and forth indicating his conuslink is not working properly. The gill officer shakes his gills in disgust and heads for the pore of the ampulla, giving his aide an annoyed look.

He clammands, "Take over. We've got a bad transfinner. I'll see what I can do."

As the gill officer approaches the ampulla pore, it slides open revealing the towering Unagibacca. The gill officer, in a momentary state of shock, stumbles backward. With a gill-chilling howl, the giant Wookieel flattens the officer with one blow. The aide immediately reaches for his laserbean pistol, but is blasted by a disguised Prawn, bottled as an Imperial saketrooper. Zen Wasabi and the roebots enter the ampulla quickly followed by Luke, also bottled as a saketrooper. Luke quickly removes his cap.

Luke yells at Prawn, "You know, between his howling and your blasting everything in sight, it's a wonder the whole battle station doesn't know we're here."

Prawn snaps back, "Bring them on! I prefer a straight fight to all this sneaking around! I feel like a shrimp in a bottle!"

Luke looks over at him and says, "You are... a shrimp in a bottle."

The sake bottle cap quickly spun to a rest after clinking my mom's dish. Unfortunately, this got the attention of my mom. Fortunately, she was engaged in my father's conversation with our sushi bar neighbor at the time of the clink. She was confused as she looked down, still in conversation, and quickly dismissed the cap. She must've thought it simply fell off the sake bottle in front of her dish. She picked it up off the bar and continued talking as she felt past the soy sauce bottle to place it loosely onto the sake bottle. Whew, a narrow escape.

I looked back over my shoulder at the tall, dark man. He sat there incredibly still. His dishes were cleared by one of the waitresses who glanced at him. He ignored her completely and simply continued to observe the sushi bar, quietly, with a stern look on his face.

Still in the ampulla, Soy-3PO informs the crew that they have found access to the Death Starfish brain, "We found the brain nerve ending, sir."

Zen Wasabi feeds some information into the brain and an anatomical drawing of the Death Starfish appears on the brain membrane. He begins to inspect it carefully. Soy-3PO and Miso-D2 look over the nerve control panel. Miso-D2 finds something that makes him whistle wildly.

Zen suggests, "Plug in. He should be able to interpret the entire Imperial brain network."

A strand of seaweed emerges from Miso-D2's bowl and punches into the brain interface nerve and the vast Imperial brain network comes to life, feeding him information. After a few moments, he burps *something and then gurgles.*

Soy-3PO interprets for Miso-D2 and says, "He says he's found the main brain to power the tractor bean that's holding the spacefish here. He'll try to make the precise location appear on the membrane."

The brain membrane flashes readouts. Zen Wasabi quickly studies the data on the membrane.

Zen informs the crew, "I don't think you minnows can help. I must go alone."

Prawn quips back, "Whatever you say. I've done more than I bargained for on this trip already."

Luke speaks to Zen, "I want to go with you."

Zen says, "Be patient, Luke. Stay and watch over the soyds."

"But he can..."

Zen interrupts, "They must be delivered safely or other platters and stacks of plates will suffer the same fate as Abaloneraan. Your destiny lies along a different path than mine. The Rice will be with you... always... because it's sticky!"

Just at that moment, Junichi-san came by to pick up some loose dishes from in front of my dad, then advanced toward the edamame bowl that now held the empty edamame husks. As I saw this, I quickly took my chopsticks, scrapped them through the small pile of wasabi on my dish and smeared it onto the edamame dish, just as his hand reached the other side. He was startled and nearly dropped the other dish he took from my dad. He looked at me with a furrowed brow and sucked his teeth as he pulled the edamame bowl away. My mom interrupted this and asked Junichi-san for some more edamame when he had a chance. Junichi-san bowed at her and then leered at me out of the corner of his eye as he made his way into the kitchen through the noren curtains. I just smiled as sarcastically as I could and shrugged my shoulders.

As I looked behind me, I noticed the tall, dark man raise his dark eyebrows and make a quick note in his notebook.

Zen adjusts the chopsabers on his belt and silently moves out of the ampulla clammand area, then disappears down a long grey hallway. Unagibacca barks a rather raw sounding comment and Prawn shakes his head in agreement.

Prawn agrees, "Soy, you said it, Unagi."

Prawn looks at Luke and asks, "Where did you dig up that old root?"

He responds, "Zen is a great paste."

"Yeah, great at getting us into trouble."

Luke retorts, "I didn't hear you give any ideas..."

Prawn continues, "Well, anything would be better than just hanging

around waiting for him to pick us up…"
Luke interjects, "Who do you think…"

My mom then surprised me and called over Hiroshi-san and asked him what type of rolls he recommended. Hiroshi-san came over and thought about it. He said the spicy tuna tempura maki were most excellent and would nicely offset the edamame, karei, and unagi. She agreed immediately and ordered six rolls, probably thinking my father would share more with the neighboring customer over more sake. I found it odd that she had agreed to tempura maki. She typically didn't like anything deep fried but maybe she had just ordered it for my dad.

Suddenly, Miso-D2 begins to whistle and burst steam. Luke goes over to him and asks about what he found.
Soy-3PO answers, "I'm afraid I'm not quite sure, sir. He says 'I found her', and keeps repeating, 'She's here'."
"Well, who… who has he found?"
Miso-D2 whistles a frantic reply.
Soy-3PO responds, "Princess Maki."
Luke questions, "The princess? She's here?"
Prawn overhears and interrupts, "Princess? What's going on?"
Soy-3PO answers Luke, "Level five. Detention block A-A-23. I'm afraid she's scheduled to be deep fried."
Luke responds, "Oh, no! We've got to do something!"
Prawn asks again irritatedly, "What are you talking about?"
Luke informs Prawn, "The soyd belongs to her. She's the one in the message… We've got to help her."
Prawn adamantly states, "Now look. Don't get any funny ideas. The old root wants us to wait right here."
Luke explains, "But he didn't know she was here. Look, will you just find a way back into the detention block?"
Prawn stubbornly replies, "I'm not going anywhere."
"They're going to deep fry her! Look, a few minutes ago you said you didn't want to just wait here to be captured. Now all you want to do is stay," implores Luke.
Prawn stares blankly at Luke and says, "Marching into the detention area is not what I had in mind."
"But they're going to fry her!"
Prawn offers, "Better her than me…"
Luke thinks for a second, realizes how shellfish Prawn is, and then blurts out, "She's rich."
Unagibacca growls.
Prawn inquires somewhat interested now, "Rich?"

Luke goes on, "Yes. Rich, powerful! Listen, if you were to rescue her, the reward would be..."

Prawn interrupts, "What?"

"Well, more than you can imagine."

Prawn informs Luke, "I don't know. I can imagine quite a bit!"

Luke promises, "You'll get it!"

Prawn looks him in the eyes and says, "I better!"

"You will..."

Prawn says, "Alright, soy. But you'd better be right about this."

Luke nods confidently.

I decided to roll up my straw wrapper into two connected circles and made them look like a pair of handcuffs... uh, fincuffs? Then I placed these onto the unagi still on my dish. I took the cap from the sake bottle and put it over the prawn also still on my dish.

Prawn asks, "What's your plan?"

Luke thinks and starts, "Uh... Soy-3PO, fin me those binders there will you?"

Luke moves toward Unagibacca with electronic fincuffs, looks up at Unagibacca and says, "Okay. Now I'm going to put these on you."

Unagibacca lets out a very aggressive growl aimed at Luke.

Luke gives the binders sheepishly to Prawn Solo and says, "Okay. Prawn, you put these on."

Prawn looks at Unagibacca and says, "Don't worry, Unagi. I think I know what he has in mind."

The Wookieel has a worried and nervous look on his face as Prawn binds him with the electronic fincuffs.

Soy-3PO asks Luke, "Master Luke, sir! Pardon me for asking... but, ah... what should Miso-D2 and I do if we're discovered here?"

Luke replies, "Lock the pore!"

Prawn looks Soy-3PO up and down and adds, "And hope they don't have laserbean blasters."

Soy-3PO looks down at the ground and says, "That isn't very reassuring."

Luke and Prawn put on their armored saketrooper bottles and caps and start off into the giant Imperial Death Starfish.

Our neighboring customer called Hiroshi-san over and ordered some yellowfish sushi called buri. I slid my small plate carrying the prawn, the atsuage, and the unagi across the bar in front of my mom, navigating around the other dishes in front of her. She was laughing at my father's story again and not really paying any attention to me or her food. I reached over through my mom's dishes and clinked my dish on the starfish platter holding the gai sakamushi.

My mother looked down, saw me basically leaning over her dishes and asked "What are you doing, honey? Do you want some clams?"

I quickly responded by shaking my head back and forth.

"Well, then why are you putting your dish by your father's gai sakamushi? I'm sure he'll share with you."

I just looked at her sheepishly and pulled my plate back, starting to navigate around the dishes in front of her in reverse. Smiled and shrugged.

My father then called out, "Right, honey? Right?!"

She quickly turned and responded as if on autopilot, "Of course, dear! Of course," and swiftly moved on to support the on-going conversation topic at hand of which she was barely aware.

Junichi-san returned with a new bowl full of edamame and hesitated to put it down in front of my mom as he peered over our heads at the tall, dark man who was now scribbling more notes in his notebook.

Prawn and Luke try to look inconspicuous in their sake bottle armor as they wait for an elevator to arrive. Saketroopers, Imperial Buricrats, and roebots bustle about, ignoring the trio completely. Only a few passersby give the giant Wookieel a curious glance. FInally, a small elevator arrives and the trio enters. An Imperial Buricrat races to get aboard as well but is signaled away by Prawn. The pore to the pod-like elevator slides closed and the elevator car takes off through an artery.

Several Imperial officers walk through the wide main passageway of the Death Starfish. They pass several saketroopers and a soy roebot similar to Soy-3PO but with a cap that looked like an insect. At the far end of the hallway, a passing flash of Zen Wasabi appears, then disappears down a small hallway. His appearance is so fleeting that it is herd to tell if he is real or just an illusion. No one in the hallway seems to notice him.

Luke and Prawn step forward to exit the elevator, but the pore slides open behind them. The giant Wookieel and his two guards turn and enter the old grey security station now before them. Guards and laserbean gates are everywhere.

Prawn whispers to Luke under his breath, "This is not going to work."

Luke, near panic, replies, "Why didn't you say so before?"

Prawn retorts, "I did say so!"

A tall, grim looking Imperial seigo officer approaches the trio and asks, "Where are you taking this… thing?"

Unagibacca growls a bit at the remark but Prawn nudges him to shut up.

Luke offers, "Prisoner transfer from Block one-one-three-eight."
The officer replies, "I wasn't notified. I'll have to clear it."

As I brought the dish holding the prawn, atsuage, and unagi back, it clinked against the sake bottle at the edge of the bar and the unagi fell off the plate and headed for the floor. With cat-like reflexes, I attempted to catch it before it fell too far and was successful. However, as I did this, my elbow hit the fresh bowl of edamame in front of my mom. The edamame spilled out across the bar and flew onto the various plates and bottles on the bar in front of us, making a rather large mess. I looked around somewhat embarrassed and locked eyes with the tall, dark man. He grimaced toward me as if he were disgusted with me. I immediately got the sense that this man did not like kids. Actually, I couldn't determine if he actually liked anything at all.

The officer goes back to his console membrane and begins to pulse in the information to the Death Starfish brain. There are only three other saketroopers in the area. Luke and Prawn survey the situation, checking all of the alarms, laserbean gates, and cameras. Prawn unfastens one of Unagibacca's fincuffs and tips his bottle cap to Luke as if to imply they have nothing to lose. Suddenly, Unagibacca jumps up and lets out with one of his loudest growls. He grabs Prawn's laserbean rifle.
Prawn calls out, "Look out! He's loose!"
Luke yells, "He's going to pull us all apart!"
Prawn yells at the nearby saketroopers, "Go get him!"
The startled saketroopers are momentarily dumbfounded. Luke and Prawn have already pulled out their laserbean pistols and are blasting away at the terrifying Wookieel. Their barrage of laserbean fire misses Unagibacca, but hits the cameras, laserbean gate controls, and the Imperial saketroopers. Prawn rushes to the conuslink system, which is screeching questions about what is going on. He quickly checks the brain membrane readout.
Prawn says, "We've got to find out which digestive gland this princess of yours is in. Here it is… gland twenty-one-eight-seven. You go get her. I'll hold them here."
Luke races down one of the digestive gland corridors.
Prawn speaks into the buzzing conuslink, "Everything is under control. Situation normal."
The voice on the conuslink asks, "What happened?"
Prawn looks about and says, "Uh… had a slight weapons malfunction. But… uh… everything's perfectly all right now. We're fine. We're all fine here, now. Thank you. How are you?"

The voice replies, "We're sending a squad case 0up."

Prawn responds quickly, "Uh... uh... negative! We have a pyloric stomach leak here now. Give us a few minutes to lock it down."

The voice questions, "Who is this? What's your operating number?"

Prawn blasts the conuslink with his laserbean pistol and it explodes.

Prawn quips, "Boring conversation anyway." He yells down the digestive gland corridor, "Luke! We're going to have company!"

My mom gazed at me with a rather disgusted and disappointed look. I smiled sheepishly. She just shook her head and resigned herself to a long night of dealing with a misbehaving son with a hyperactive imagination and an overly jovial husband with a hyperactive urge to tell elaborate stories over sake. I glanced back at the tall, dark man and he too shook his head ever so slowly from side to side too, his eyes never faltering from their unblinking stare in my direction. I was sufficiently creeped out.

8 THE CLAMBASSADOR'S RESCUE

My mom urged me to clean up the mess I had made with the spilled edamame by motioning with her hand toward individual pieces scattered along the bar and on various dishes. I hurriedly got to work on picking all of these up and placed them into the bowl. They were still relatively warm and since they were still in husks, the beans weren't ruined.

Hiroshi-san came up to the bar, peered over the counter, and asked, "What happened here, Billy-san?"

I smiled sheepishly and my mom stated, "Oh, you know, Hiroshi-san... boys will be boys. I guess he got a little too excited over the delicious edamame."

She giggled. Hiroshi-san smiled with doubt on his lips, bowed, and placed a narrow serving board containing the spicy tuna tempura maki roll onto the bar in front of us.

As I cleaned up the last of the edamame from the bar surface, I squeezed one and the beans within exploded out of the warm husk toward the large starfish serving tray containing the gai sakamushi that my father was clearly enjoying. One bean ricocheted off the side of the starfish tray and landed on the spicy tuna tempura maki roll tray. No one seemed to notice, thankfully.

The tall, dark man sitting behind us read over his notes in his small notebook, nodded to himself, and then closed the notebook with confidence, seemingly satisfied with himself for something.

My mother grabbed a maki roll and placed it on my dish next to the atsuage and then scolded me a bit for not eating anything. I grabbed the atsuage with my chopsticks and started to lead it to my mouth as if I was about to eat it and as she turned away, I placed it back on my dish. Going through these motions made me realize that I hadn't yet received my kushi order, yet again! I seriously began to think that Hiroshi-san wouldn't actually start cooking the kushi until I asked about it a second time. Perhaps he hoped this strategy would encourage me to try some sushi.

Luke Soywalker stops in front of one of the digestive glands and blasts the cell wall of the gland with his laserbean pistol. When the steam clears, Luke sees the dazzling young princess-seanator. She had been sleeping and is now looking at him with an uncomprehending look in her red eyes as she rolled over. Luke is stunned by her incredible beauty and stands staring at her with his mouth hanging open.

Princess Maki finally asks, "Aren't you a little short to be a saketrooper?"

The bottled Luke takes off his cap and says, "What? Oh... the uniform. I'm Luke Soywalker. I'm here to rescue you."

"You're who?"

Luke straightens up a bit and further explains, "I'm here to rescue you. I've got your Miso-D2 unit. I'm here with Zen Wasabi."

Princess Maki looks encouraged and asks, "Zen Wasabi is here?Where is he?"

Luke urges her to come with him.

The tall, dark man scanned the sushi bar from wall to wall with scrutinizing eyes. He then tucked his small notebook into his shirt pocket and stood up. He walked over to the sushi bar and stood there between the neighboring customer and my father, rudely ignoring the fact they had been in the middle of talking to one another. My father looked up at him and appeared like he wanted to say something but realized the tall, dark man was rather intense. I suspected my father quickly realized that the fun he was having this night would come to an abrupt end if he had confronted the tall, dark man so he shrugged his shoulders, stared ahead and took a sip of sake. The neighboring customer did exactly the same thing.

Hiroshi-san, sensing something was wrong at the sushi bar, came out of the kitchen and cautiously approached the tall, dark man with his head cocked to one side in a confused but worried manner. The tall, dark man said nothing. He simply took a card out of his pocket and handed it to Hiroshi-san revealing the tattoo on his arm of a black starfish. Hiroshi-san hesitantly took the card, glanced at it quickly and confusedly looked up at the tall, dark man. By the time he had done so, the tall, dark man had turned his back to the bar and started walking toward the exit. Hiroshi-san held up the card and started to say something to the man, but he had already left out of the front door.

Hiroshi-san looked nervously at his customers, then back at the card, and forced a smile, bowing quickly to anyone who might've been looking at him. He placed the card in his apron and returned to the kitchen hurriedly, visibly filled with concern.

Squid Vader oozes across the room as Grand Moff Tarako sits at the far end of the conference napkin.

Squid Vader says, "He is here..."

Tarako asks curiously, "Obi-Wan Wasabi?! What makes you think so?"

Vader replies, "A stickiness in the Rice. The last time I felt it was in the presence of my old master."

Tarako reasons, "Surely, he must be fried by now."

"Don't underestimate the power of the Rice."

Tarako explains, "The Red-Eye are extinct. Their roots have dried up across the oceanverse. You, my friend, are all that's left of their starchiness."

There is a quiet buzz on the conuslink.

Tarako calls out, "Yes?"

A voice on the conuslink states, "Grand Moff Tarako, we have an emergency alert in digestive gland block A A-twenty-three."

Tarako exclaims, "The princess! Put all sections on alert!"

Squid Vader reiterates, "Obi-Wan is here. The Rice is with him."

Tarako states, "If you are right, he must not be allowed to escape."

Squid Vader informs Tarako, "Escape is not his plan. I must face him alone."

Hiroshi-san came back out of the kitchen and asked my father if he cared for more sake. My mother raised her hand and started saying she thought he had had enough. My father raised his hand even higher and debated this by burping, excusing himself, and then stating that he had to have one more bottle in order to be a most gracious host to our new friend. He couldn't remember his neighbor's name so he slurred something and ended it with "san". The neighbor didn't seem to mind. He had a seemingly permanent grin on his face. My mother conceded and nodded to Hiroshi-san with a heavy sigh and said, "But the small one". He bowed with a smirk and went to the shelves to retrieve my father's favorite type of sake, in a small bottle.

He opened the bottle and placed it in front of my father. My father raised his ochoko, a sake cup, to Hiroshi-san and thanked my mom for her concession. He then poured some sake for his neighbor. The neighbor took the bottle and reciprocated. They raised their ochokos and drank together. My mother placed the bottle in front of her, between the serving dish holding the spicy tuna tempura maki and my plate that still

94

held a piece of unagi, prawn, and atsuage.

I took an edamame and squeezed it, aiming at the sake bottle. Two of the beans shot out and both hit the bottle ricocheting onto the bar. Boys will be boys... I guess.

At the entrance to the radial canal, a hallway separating the digestive gland cell walls, an ominous buzzing sound is heard on the other side of the ring canal pore.

Prawn Solo calls out, "Unagi!"

Unagibacca responds with a deep growling noise.

Prawn continues, "Get behind me! Get behind me!"

A series of explosions knock a hole in the ring canal pore through which several Imperial saketroopers begin to emerge. Prawn and Unagibacca fire laserbean pistols at them through the steam and beans. They turn and make their way down the radial canal, meeting up with Luke and Princess Maki rushing toward them.

My mom looked into my eyes sternly and said, "Billy, just eat, please. It will be a long enough night and I don't need a hungry and grumpy 10 year old to go with a overjoyed and tipsy 40 year old." I looked at her sheepishly, grabbed my chopsticks again and grabbed the prawn on my plate. I raised it to my mouth, hesitantly, grinned at her, and nibbled at the edge of the prawn. It was not appetizing at all. My mother turned back to keep an eye on my father so I quickly placed the prawn behind the unagi on my dish, so that it might be difficult for my mother to see it if she glanced over to check on what I might have actually eaten. I then informed her that I hadn't received the kushi I ordered. She motioned over to Hiroshi-san and inquired about it. He looked confused and then went into the kitchen to check on it.

Prawn informs, "Can't get out that way."

Princess Maki replies, "Looks like you managed to cut off our only escape route."

"Maybe you'd like it back in your digestive gland, Your Gai-ness," retorts Prawn sarcastically.

Luke takes a small conuslink transfinner from his belt as they continue to exchange laserbean fire with the saketroopers making their way down the canal.

Luke calls out into the conuslink transfinner, "Soy-3PO! Soy-3PO!"

Soy-3PO responds over the conuslink, "Yes, sir?"

Luke explains, "We've been cut off! Are there any other ways out of the radial canal?"

The noise of the laserbean battle rises over the conuslink tidemissions.

Luke asks, "What was that? I didn't copy."

Back in the ampulla, Soy-3PO waddles back and forth in the nerve control center as Miso-D2 burps and gurgles.

Soy-3PO yells into the small conuslink transfinner, "I said, all systems have been alerted to your presence, sir. The ring canal entrance seems to be the only way in or out. All other information on your level is restricted."

Someone begins banging on the ampulla wall. A saketrooper calls out as he continues to bang. Soy-3PO begins to panic.

My father enjoyed his sake with the neighboring customer and continued to share many stories. My father finished the gai sakamushi and placed the starfish serving tray onto the top shelf of the sushi bar in front of my mom to make more room in front of him. He smiled at her and mouthed a thank you to her. She nodded her approval and excused herself while placing her hand over my dad's shoulder. She stood up from her stool and went to the restroom.

I took this opportunity to place the prawn, the unagi, the atsuage, and the spicy tuna tempura maki roll on my dish into one of the arms of the large starfish serving tray. One by one, I placed them with my chopsticks onto the serving tray in hopes that Hiroshi-san or Junichi-san would grab the tray and take it to the kitchen before my mom returned.

I looked at the bowl of edamame and realized that this was likely the only food I would really be able to eat tonight since I really did not want to eat any of the sushi and it looked bleak for getting my kushi any time soon. I took a handful of the edamame and placed them on my dish and popped the beans into my mouth by squeezing the husks. I then threw the empty husks onto the sushi I placed into the starfish serving tray and tried to cover them up. I filled my mouth with several of these beans and after 10 or so husks placed conveniently over my sushi, I started choking on the beans. I tried chewing them quickly, but there were so many of them that I started to gag and cough. Just then, my mom came back from the restroom and I coughed so hard that my mouthful of half-chewed edamame beans started spewing out. I stood up coughing and sprayed beans all over the starfish serving tray. My mom ran over to me, very concerned and patted my back. My father stopped talking and stood up to also come to my assistance. I coughed one more time, gagged, and swallowed what remained in my mouth.

My father gave me my glass of water and said, "Son, here... drink this. You ok?"

My very concerned mom kept patting my back asking if I was ok. I was. She grabbed a napkin and started wiping my mouth.

I drank the water and sat back down, nodding, coughing and said, "I'm ok guys. Sorry. I'm ok."

My father called over to Junichi-san as my mother began lecturing me on stuffing my mouth with too much food and asked Junichi-san to remove the serving tray and grab me some more water. In all of the commotion of my choking, my plan had actually worked. Junichi-san grabbed the starfish serving tray carrying all of my sushi to the kitchen with it unbeknownst to my parents. I drank more water and smiled between coughs and assured my parents that I was fine.

Luke and Princess Maki crouch together in an alcove near the Death Starfish's ring canal entrance for protection as they continue to exchange laserbean fire with the saketroopers. Prawn Solo and Unagibacca are barely able to keep the saketroopers at bay at the far end of the hallway. The laserbean fire is very intense, and steam fills the canal hallway by the digestive gland cells.

Luke calls out, "There isn't any other way out."

Prawn replies, "I can't hold them off forever! Now what?"

Princess Maki criticizes, "This is some rescue. When you came in here, didn't you have a plan for getting out? It's like low tide and we're pinned behind a rock high on the beach."

Prawn points his claw at Luke and says, "He's the brains, sweetheart."

Luke manages a sheepish grin and shrugs as he tries to explain, "Well, I didn't... uh..."

Princess Maki grabs Luke's laserbean pistol and fires at a small gland in the cell wall next to Prawn, almost frying him.

Prawn yells, "What on land are you doing?!"

She replies, "Somebody has to save our rolls. Into the garbage chute, you shellfish."

On the way to the kitchen, Junichi-san scraped out the contents of the starfish serving tray into the trash can behind the bar, next to the entrance to the kitchen just across from where I sat. I watched as the maki roll, atsuage, prawn, and unagi fell into the trash can followed by edamame husks and sake broth. I was shocked that Junichi-san did not ask my parents about the uneaten sushi in the serving dish. He was clearly off his game, probably distracted by the tall, dark man's visit.

Princess Maki jumps through the narrow opening as Prawn and Unagibacca look on in amazement. Unagibacca sniffs the garbage chute and growls at Prawn.

Prawn looks at Unagi and says, "Get in there you big, slimy eel! I don't care what you smell! Get in there and don't worry about it."

Prawn gives him a slap with his tail and the Wookieel disappears into the tiny opening. Luke and Prawn continue firing their laserbean pistols as they work their way toward the opening.

Prawn looks over at Luke and yells, "Wonderful roll she is! Either I'm going to fry her or I'm beginning to like her. Get in there!"

Luke ducks under laserbean fire from the saketroopers as he jumps into the darkness. Prawn fires off a couple of quick blasts creating a steamy cover, then slides into the chute himself and is gone. Prawn tumbles into the large room filled with garbage and muck. Luke is already stumbling around looking for an exit. He finds a small rip in the large, thick, black plastic bag and struggles to get it open. It won't budge.

Prawn addresses Princess Maki, "Oh! The garbage chute was a really wonderful idea. What an incredible smell you've discovered! Let's get out of here! Get away from there…"

Luke yells out, "No! Wait!"

Junichi-san continued into the kitchen with the serving dish and put it on the counter by the sink. I took an edamame from the bowl in front of my mom, made sure she wasn't looking and squeezed the pod at the garbage can. A rather large bean launched from the husk into the air in an arc and hit the rim of the garbage can, bounced off the bar cabinet, and landed back into the garbage can. No one saw this.

Prawn draws his laserbean pistol and fires at the small rip in the large, thick plastic bag. The laserbean ricochets wildly around the small compartment. Everyone dives for cover in the garbage as the bean explodes almost on top of them. Princess Maki climbs out of the garbage with a rather grim look on her face, her rolls dripping with muck.

Luke says, "Will you forget it? I already tried it. It's plastically sealed!"

Princess Maki chimes in, "Put that thing away! You're going to get us all fried."

Prawn, a bit disturbed, retorts, "Absolutely, Your Rollship. Look, I had everything under control until you led us down here. You know, it's not going to take them long to figure out what happened to us." Princess Maki looks at Prawn and says, "It could be worse."

Hiroshi-san came over to check in with my father to make sure the meal was to his liking. He actually said it was but that I needed my kushi. Hiroshi-san said it would be ready in a few minutes. He then mentioned a special meal.

He said, "Tom-san, I remember last time you wanted a special dish and I made you the Starfish. Maybe not the best experience. Tonight, I have very unique dish. It is called odori-don."

My father asked what odori-don was. Hiroshi-san then explained that it is actually simply a live squid with the head removed, served on top of a bowl of sushi rice and sashimi prepared from the head and liver of the squid. My father apparently didn't have enough sake to be brave enough to try this dish. He asked a few more questions about it but ultimately declined the offer. Hiroshi-san laughed and said only one customer tonight accepted his offer for it, a man from Japan only visiting for one week. He was celebrating something with his friend. Junichi-san overheard the conversation and added, "Yes. Specia-er... ah... Specia..ell dish... though they not finish." As he said this, he pointed to the trash can. Everyone smiled and laughed, including the neighboring customer, well engaged in conversation with my father. Apparently, the odori-don is a rather difficult dish to eat. If you don't eat it properly by wrapping the tentacles around your chopsticks and working to swallow it whole, the tentacles will writhe and wrap around your face, possibly even expand in your mouth or worse, in your throat, causing one to choke.

A loud, horrible moan works its way up from the murky depths at the bottom of the garbage compartment. Unagibacca lets out a terrified howl and begins to back away. Prawn and Luke stand fast with their laserbean pistols drawn. The Wookieel is cowering near one of the walls. Odori-don, a squid-like creature at the bottom of the garbage, thought to already be eaten, writhes below.

Prawn speaks up, "Uh... It's worse!"

Luke states the obvious, "There's something still alive in here!"

Prawn tries to deny the obvious, "That's your imagination."

Luke re-emphasizes, "Uh... something just moved past my crust! Look! Did you see that?!"

Prawn looks around.

"What?"

Luke yells out, "Help!"

Suddenly, Luke is yanked under the garbage.

Prawn calls out, "Luke! Luke! Luke!"

Prawn Solo tries to get to Luke. Luke surfaces with a gasp of air and a thrashing of his crust body. A slimy squid-like tentacle is wrapped around his soy body.

Princess Maki calls out to him with concern, "Luke!"

She extends a long kushi kebab toward him and instructs him to grab a hold of it.

Luke yells out to Prawn, "Blast it, will you?! My gun's jammed."

Prawn asks, "Where?"
Luke yells, "Anywhere! Oh!"
Prawn Solo fires his laserbean pistol downward. Luke is pulled back into the muck by the slimy tentacle. Prawn calls out to him again.

Hiroshi-san asked Junichi-san to empty the small trash can into the compactor in the kitchen. He bowed and immediately picked up the trash can and brought it into the kitchen, where I saw him lift the can and dump it into a trash compactor that sat by the door to the back alley. He closed the lid to the compactor and pressed a red button on the front panel. The compactor started to rumble and squeeze the trash into a smaller cube. It must have been cheaper for Moto Sushi to minimize their waste that they threw away each night into the large trash bin in the back alley.

Suddenly, the walls of the garbage receptacle shudder and move in a couple of millimeters. Then everything is deathly quiet. Prawn and Princess Maki give each other a worried look as Unagibacca howls in the corner. With a rush of bubbles and muck, Luke suddenly bobs to the surface.
Princess Maki yells, "Grab him!"
Luke seems to be released by the squid-like thing.
Princess Maki asks Luke what happened.
Luke replies, "I don't know. It just let go of me and disappeared."
Prawn looks around at the muck and the walls and says, "I've got a very bad feeling about this."
Before anyone can say anything the walls begin to rumble and edge toward the Rebels.
Luke screams, "The walls are moving!"
Princess Maki orders, "Don't just stand there! Try to brace it with something!"
They place used kushi kebabs, chopsticks, and toothpicks between the closing walls, but they are simply snapped and bent as the giant trash compactor rumbles on. The situation does not look good and panic begins to settle in with the crew.
Luke gets an idea and pulls out his transfinner and calls, "Soy-3PO! Come in Soy-3PO! Soy-3PO! Where could he be?!"

Junichi-san returned the small trash can back to its original position. In so doing though, he hit the shelf containing his neatly ordered sake and soy bottles with the rim of the trash can. The bottles started rattling. Four of the sake bottles seemed to wobble near the edge of the shelf. Junichi-san stopped frozen with fear and braced himself anticipating a crashing sound as he hesitantly glanced upwards, fully expecting to see it rain sake bottles.

A soft buzzer and the muted voice of Luke calling out for Soy-3PO can be heard on Soy-3PO's transfinner, which is sitting on the deserted brain nerve console. Miso-D2 and Soy-3PO are nowhere in sight. Suddenly, there is a great explosion and the pore to the control tube foot flies across the floor. Four saketroopers with weapons drawn enter the chamber.

One saketrooper sees to the fried Imperial officer while another pushes a button on the nerve membrane console and the supply air sac slides open. Soy-3PO and Miso-D2 are inside. Miso-D2 follows his golden companion out into the office.

Soy-3PO excitedly states, "They're madfish! They're heading for the prison level. If you hurry, you might catch them."

One saketrooper orders another to stay guard and orders the other two to follow him. The saketroopers hustle off down the hallway.

Soy-3PO calls out to Miso-D2, "Come on!"

The saketrooper guard aims a laserbean blaster at them. Soy-3PO explains, "Oh! All this excitement has overheated the tofu of my counterpart here. If you don't mind, I'd like to take him down to the kitchen for a refill."

The saketrooper guard approves with a nod of his cap and Soy-3PO, with Miso-D2 in tow, hurries out the pore after grabbing his transfinner.

Back in the kitchen, the noise of the trash compactor continued and started getting louder. Junichi-san finally reacted and started focusing on keeping the sake bottles from falling off the shelf.

As the walls rumble closer, the room in the garbage compactor gets smaller and smaller. Unagibacca is whining and trying to hold a wall back with his giant eel head. Prawn Solo is leaning back against the other wall. Garbage is snapping and popping. Luke is trying to reach Soy-3PO on the transfinner.

Luke yells, "Soy-3PO! Come in, Soy-3PO! Soy-3PO!"

Prawn and Princess Maki try to brace the contracting walls with a chopstick. Princess Maki begins to sink into the trash.

Prawn calls out to her, "Get to the top!"

Princess Maki replies in a bit of panic, "I can't!"

Luke continues yelling into the transfinner, "Where could he be? Soy-3PO! Soy-3PO, will you come in?!"

I placed the soy sauce bottle and the miso bowl in front of me up on top of the sushi bar, looking over towards the replaced trash can.

Soy-3PO and Miso-D2 arrive at a service panel in the main forward bay of the Death Starfish. Soy-3PO addresses Miso-D2, "They aren't here! Something must have happened to them. See if they've been captured."

Miso-D2 carefully plugs his seaweed from beneath his cover bowl into a cell wall socket and a complex array of burps, whistles, and glugs spew from the tiny roebot. Soy-3PO looks around and encourages Miso-D2 to hurry.

The trash compactor continued to rumble even louder and even my mom glanced over to the kitchen to see what the noise was. Junichi-san saw us look into the kitchen, reacting to the sounds and told us it would stop soon.

The walls of the trash compactor are only centimeters apart. Princess Maki and Prawn Solo are braced against the walls. The princess is fryghtened. They look at each other. Princess Maki reaches out her nori and attaches tightly to Prawn's shell. She's terrifried and suddenly groans as she feels the first crushing pressure against her rolls.

Prawn quips, "One thing's for sure. We're all going to be a lot thinner!"

He yells at Princess Maki to get on top of the trash again. She yells back at him that she's trying but it is clear she is starting to really panic.

Junichi-san saw that I placed the soy sauce bottle and miso bowl on the sushi bar. He came over and asked if there was something wrong with the soy sauce and if I was done with my miso soup. I just shook my head side to side. He shrugged and went into the kitchen.

Soy-3PO talks to Miso-D2 as he remains connected to the service panel, "Thank goodness they haven't found them! Where could they be?"

Miso-D2 frantically blurps something to Soy-3PO.

Soy-3PO responds, "Use the transfinner? Oh my, I forgot I turned it off!"

Meanwhile, in the trash compactor, Luke is lying on his side, trying to keep his head above the rising ooze. Luke's transfinner begins to buzz and he rips it off his utility belt.

Soy-3PO hears muffled sounds of Luke's voice over the transfinner, but not distinctly.

Soy-3PO calls out, "Are you there, sir?"

Luke cries out, "Soy-3PO!"

Soy-3PO starts to explain, "We've had some problems..."

Luke interrupts, "Will you shut up and listen to me?! Shut down all garbage mashers on the detention level, will you?!" Do you copy?"

He continues loudly, "Shut down all the garbage mashers on the detention level!"

Soy-3PO addresses Miso-D2, "No. Shut them all down! Hurry!"

Soy-3PO holds his cap in agony as he hears the incredible screaming and hollering from Luke's transfinner.

Junichi-san entered the kitchen and presses the trash compactor button, turning it off and stopping the annoying noise.

Soy-3PO implores Miso-D2, "Listen to them! They're frying! Miso-D2! Curse my glass body! I wasn't fast enough. It's all my fault! My poor master!"

Luke calls out very excitedly, "Soy-3PO! We're alright!

The screaming and hollering is the sound of joyous relief. The walls have stopped moving. Prawn, Unagibacca, and Princess Maki embrace above the trash.

Luke speaks into the transfinner again, "We're alright! You did great! We're just a little trashed."

Luke moves to the garbage maintenance hatch, looking for a number and calls to Soy-3PO over the transfinner, "Hey... hey, open the garbage maintenance hatch on unit number... where are we?" Prawn speaks into the transfinner, "Three-two-six-eight-two-seven."

Junichi-san returned to the sushi bar to prepare some fresh wasabi for another customer. I asked Junichi-san if my kushikatsu was done cooking. He looked at me as he finished placing the wasabi on a dish and then carried the grater tools into the kitchen and placed them on one arm of the starfish serving dish by the kitchen sink. Some wasabi remnants fell into the dish.

Obi-Wan Wasabi enters a humming service canal in the heart of the Death Starfish that powers the huge tractor bean. The radial canal seems to be a decimeter deep. The clacking sound of huge switching devices can be heard. The old Red-Eye edges his way along a narrow ledge leading to a control membrane that connects two large pyloric ducts. He carefully makes several adjustments in the membrane terminal and several pulses on the membrane go from red to blue.

Junichi-san then opened and checked the trash compactor to make sure there was room for more as it was a busy night at Moto Sushi. As he peered in, he saw something move and jumped back gasping a bit. Junichi-san grabbed a nearby broom and started to jab at the compacted trash. Hiroshi-san entered the kitchen and asked what Junichi-san was doing with a broom in the compactor. I heard Junichi-san say a lot of words in Japanese and Hiroshi-san responded with a puzzled look and further questions in Japanese. I then heard him ask, "Odori? The squid is still moving?"

Apparently, the remnants of the odori-don dish were still... uh, moving... in the trash, even after compacting. At least, that was what I could only assume had happened. I heard Hiroshi-san suck his teeth and recommend something in Japanese. Junichi-san pulled the broom out of the trash which now had several sushi remnants attached to it. Hiroshi-san walked out of the kitchen minutes later with my kushikatsu on a white dish and placed it in front of me. I began eating right away.

The trash compactor hatch opens. Prawn Solo, Princess Maki, Luke Soywalker and Unagibacca all exit the trash compactor onto a dirty platform made from something resembling straw. Prawn and Luke remove the saketrooper bottles currently encasing their bodies and strap on the laserbean blaster belts.

Prawn quips, "If we can just avoid any more rolled advice, we ought to be able to get out of here."

Luke smiles and scratches his head crust as he takes a laserbean blaster from Prawn and says, "Well, let's get moving."

Unagibacca begins growling and nods back down to the hatch of the trash compactor, as he hops further up the platform and then stops howling.

Prawn yells after Unagibacca, "Where are you going?"

The Odori-don bangs against the top hatch and a long, slimy tentacle works its way out of the compactor searching for a victim. Prawn aims his laserbean pistol.

Princess Maki warns Prawn, "No wait! They'll hear!"

Prawn fires his laserbean pistol at the hatch. The noise of the blast echoes relentlessly throughout the empty area. Luke simply shakes his head in disgust.

Prawn yells to Unagibacca, "Come here, you big coward!"

Unagibacca shakes his head from side to side.

Prawn yells again frustrated, "Unagi! Come here!"

Princess Maki interrupts, "Listen. I don't know who you are, or where you came from, but from now on, you do as I tell you. Okay?"

Prawn, taken aback by the remark, replies, "Look, your Starchfulness, let's get one thing straight! I take orders from one sushiform! Me!"

Maki looks disgusted and says, "It's a wonder you're still raw." She looks at Unagibacca in front of her and says, "Will somebody get this big, swimming fish bait out of my way?"

Prawn watches her start away. He looks at Luke and says, "No reward is worth this."

They follow her, moving swiftly across the area.

Junichi-san grabbed the broom again and looked into the compacted trash to make sure the odori-don was dead. When he raised the broom handle up high enough to get the broom into the compactor this time, the handle hit the shelf above him that held a few extra bottles of sake. One of the bottles rattled near the edge. He quickly pulled out the broom and it hit the shelf even harder and the bottle near the edge of the shelf actually fell onto the kitchen counter below and safely landed into the starfish serving tray on the arm containing the smudge of wasabi and edamame husks.

Suddenly a pore behind Zen Wasabi slides open and a detachment of saketroopers marches to the power canal of the Death Starfish. Zen instantly slips into the shadows as an Imperial officer moves to within a few millimeters of him. The officer calls out to the troops, "Secure this area until the alert is cancelled."

All but two of the saketroopers leave. The first saketrooper asks the other if he knows what is going on. The second saketrooper suggests it might be another drill.

Zen moves around the tractor bean, watching the saketroopers as they turn their bottles away from him. Zen gestures with a grain of rice toward them as the saketroopers think they hear something in the other pyloric duct. With the help of the Rice, Zen deftly slips past the saketroopers and into the main pyloric duct.

One saketrooper asks the other, "What was that?"

His companion responds, "Oh, it's nothing. Don't worry about it."

Hiroshi-san returned to the kitchen and yelled at Junichi-san to put the broom away and to stop worrying about the trash. He explained there were many customers that needed tending and that the trash does not pay the bills. Junichi-san bowed heavily and apologetically. He was about to place the broom back into the kitchen closet when he noticed there was a bunch of sushi remnants on the broom's bristles and that it would have to be cleaned before putting it away. He leaned the broom by the wall closest to the sink as he nodded.

My father was still eating his karei and chatting with the neighboring patron as he got distracted by the swinging around of the broom in the kitchen and commented to my mom about how Junichi-san didn't seem "right" tonight. He moved the sake bottle closer to his cup and offered his neighbor more. He accepted. They drank.

Luke, Prawn, Unagibacca, and Princess Maki ooze down the empty straw platform and stop to look through a poreway and spot the Millennium Flounder spacefish a fair distance away in the hangar.

Prawn utters, "There she is."

Luke calls into his transfinner, "Soy-3PO, do you copy?"

Soy-3PO responds immediately, "For the moment. Uh, we're in the main hangar across from the spacefish."

Luke replies, "We're right across from you. Stand by."

Prawn is watching the dozen or so saketroopers stationed about the hangar and two especially near the spacefish. Princess Maki moves towards Prawn, looks at him, looks at the Millennium Flounder, looks at him again, and looks at the spacefish once more and says, "You came in that thing? You're braver than I thought."

Prawn looks at her in disgust and says, "Nice, Your Roeyal Makiness. Now come on!"

The group starts off the straw platform. They come to a narrow wooden pole section and climb it single file for a while until they come up under a large overhang. They jump onto the other side of the overhang and encounter twenty Imperial saketroopers heading toward them. Both groups are taken by surprise and stop in their tracks.

The first saketrooper in line calls out, "It's them! Blast them!"

Before even thinking, Prawn Solo draws his laserbean pistol and charges the saketroopers, firing. His laserbean blaster knocks one of the saketroopers into the air. Unagibacca follows his captain down the overhang, stepping over the fallen saketrooper now on its side, leaking sake onto the shelf.

Prawn Solo calls out to Luke and Princess Maki, "Get back to the spacefish!"

Luke calls back, "Where are you going? Come back!"

Prawn has already climbed onto the other side of the shelf and does not hear Luke.

Princess Maki says, "He certainly has courage."

Luke responds concernedly, "What good will it do us if he gets himself fried? Come on!"

Luke is furious but doesn't have time to think about it for muted alarms begin to go off down on the hangar deck. Luke and Princess Maki start off toward the spacefish hangar.

Junichi-san tended to a few customers at the sushi bar, refilling drinks and clearing plates. One customer asked for some sake so Junichi-san grabbed one of the newly delivered cases of sake near me at the end of the bar and brought the box into the kitchen. He set it down on the counter by the sink, very near the dirty starfish serving dish. He adjusted the broom along the wall near the sink then started sliding towards the box. He caught it before it hit anything and balanced it back along the wall. Unbeknownst to Junichi-san, the sushi remnants and edamame husks once attached to the broom bristles fell down the top edge of the broom, onto the broom handle, and oozed into the serving dish. He cut the sake case box open with a box cutter and took the sake bottles out one by one and set them on the counter by the sink. One clinked the starfish serving dish.

Prawn Solo chases the saketroopers down a long ambulacral ridge. He is yelling and brandishing his laserbean pistol. The saketroopers reach a dead end at some perivisceral coelom, a large cavity containing vital organs of the Death Starfish, and are forced to turn and fight. Prawn stops a few centimeters from them and assumes a definsive position. The saketroopers begin to raise their laserbean guns. Soon all ten saketroopers are moving into an attack position in front of the lone crustacean. Prawn's determined look begins to fade as the saketroopers begin to advance. Prawn Solo jumps backward as they fire beans at him.

Unagibacca storms down the same ambulacral ridge in a last-ditch attempt to save his bold captain. Suddenly, he hears the firing of laserbean guns and yelling. Around the ampullae shoots Prawn, sea-pirate extraordinaire, tail jumping for his life, followed by a host of furious saketroopers. Unagibacca turns and starts storming the other way down the ambulacral ridge too.

Luke fires his laserbean pistol wildly as he and Princess Maki rush down a narrow pyloric duct, chased by several saketroopers. They quickly reach the end of the pyloric caecam and race through an open ossicle.

Luke and Princess Maki race through the ossicle onto a narrow body wall that spans a huge, deep void that seems to go into in-fin-ity. The other arm has been retracted away from the body wall of the arm on which they sit, and Luke almost rushes into the abyss. He loses his balance off the end of the arm as Maki, behind him, takes hold of his utility belt and pulls him back.

Luke gasps, "I think we took a wrong turn."

Blasts from the saketroopers' laserbean guns explode nearby reminding them of the oncoming danger. Luke fires back at the advancing saketroopers. Princess Maki reaches over and hits a skin gill that pops the ossicle pore shut with a resounding boom, leaving them precariously perched on a short piece of arm overhang. Laserbean fire from the saketroopers continues to hit the ossicle pore.

Princess Maki yells, "There's no lock!"

Luke blasts the skin gill control with his laserbean pistol.

A proud Luke says, "That ought to hold it for a while."

Maki urges, "Quick, we've got to get across. Find the control that extends the arm."

Luke sadly informs, "Oh, I think I just bean blasted it."

Junichi-san unpacked all of the sake bottles and they kept clinking on the starfish serving dish. He checked the box and then threw the empty box by the back door in hopes that he would be able to take it out to the dumpster before Hiroshi-san saw he left it there. In the act of throwing the box, Junichi-san actually hit one of the sake bottles and toppled it onto the counter while the box squarely hit another bottle slightly further in it's trajectory and sent it flying across the kitchen onto the floor. It smashed into a thousand pieces and spilled the contents onto the floor. The liquid slowly meandered towards the floor drain.

Luke looks at the blasted arm control while the saketroopers on the opposite side of the ossicle begin making ominous drilling and pounding sounds.

Maki hears this and tells Luke, "They're coming through!"

Luke notices something on his belt, when laserbean fire hits the arm behind him. Luke aims his laserbean pistol at a saketrooper perched on a high shelf across the abyss from them. They exchange bean fire. Two more saketroopers appear on another overhanging shelf, also firing. A saketrooper is hit, and grabs at his bottle as he dramatically falls over. Another saketrooper standing on the shelf overhang is hit by Luke's laserbean fire, and plummets down into the abyss. Saketroopers move back off the arm. Luke gives the gun to Princess Maki.

Luke instructs Maki, "Here. Hold this."

Junichi-san looked around and then sheepishly looked out from the kitchen, muttering something in Japanese, hoping that Hiroshi-san didn't just see him smash a sake bottle, a full sake bottle. The restaurant was busy so he was lucky. He scurried back into the kitchen, grabbed the broom from the wall, and shook the bristles over the sink in a feeble attempt to clean them. One lone soba noodle from the trash compactor fell from the broom's bristles and landed on the starfish serving dish and spanned across two arms of the starfish. He began to hurriedly sweep up the sake mess.

Luke pulls a thin soba noodle from his utility belt. He ties two toothpicks onto one end of it in a cross shape. A saketrooper appears on a shelf overhang and fires at Luke and Maki. As Luke works with the noodle, Princess Maki returns the laserbean volley. Another saketrooper appears and fires at them, as the Princess returns his fire as well. Suddenly, the ossicle pore begins to open, revealing the bottles of more saketroopers.
Princess Maki warns, "Here they come!"

Junichi-san panicked, hearing Hiroshi-san nearby talking to a customer. He started feverishly sweeping up the broken glass and pushing the sake liquid on the floor down toward the drain in the middle of the floor. He got all the glass into a neat pile and saw Hiroshi-san approaching the kitchen. He quickly grabbed a nearby dish towel and threw it over the pile of broken glass on the floor and threw the broom to the corner of the kitchen in hopes it would land upright, leaning in the corner. It didn't. The broom had a little too much momentum and rose higher than anticipated. The broom handle hit the bottom of the opposing shelf that held a few older sake bottles. When the broom handle hit, the sake bottle on the very edge of the shelf fell off, tumbled down onto the counter, amazingly bounced without breaking and landed in the center of the floor right in front of Hiroshi-san as he entered and smashed to pieces, splashing sake everywhere.

Maki hits one of the saketroopers on the shelf above, and he falls into the abyss. Luke tosses the noodle across the abyss and it wraps itself around an outcropping of pyloric caecam. He tugs on the noodle to make sure it is secure, then grabs the Princess with his crust. Maki looks at Luke, then kisses him quickly. Luke is very surprised.
Princess Maki explains, "For luck!"
Luke responds, "Soba, so good!"
Luke pushes off and they swing across the treacherous abyss to the corresponding ossicle on the opposite arm. Just as Luke and Maki reach the far side onto the other arm, the saketroopers break through the first ossicle and begin to fire laserbeans at the escaping duo. Luke returns

the fire before ducking into the tiny pyloric duct.

Hiroshi-san said nothing. He stood in the middle of the kitchen, looking at the broken glass on the floor. He raised his arms, shaking them back and forth, not uttering a word. He looked at Junichi-san who hung his head in shame amidst an uncontrollable shiver throughout his body. Hiroshi-san started to utter something very quietly, then stopped. He looked back out of the kitchen onto his many customers and looked back at Junichi-san, looked at the glass, looked at the dishes and calmly said, "Glass. Sake. Dishes. Clean now. Next, customers!" as he pointed to each.

Junichi-san bowed deeper than I had ever seen him bow. Hiroshi-san let out a big sigh and left the kitchen. Junichi-san quickly grabbed the broom from the wall and started sweeping the floor, collecting the glass pieces into another pile on the floor. He then brushed the sake into the drain as best he could. I had never seen him move so fast. He then cleaned up both piles of glass pieces with a dust pan and small hand brush. He dumped the glass into the trash compactor, scurried back to the dishes by the sink and started to clean the starfish serving dish. Just as he was about to spray the starfish serving dish with the sink's water hose, he slipped on the sake-soaked kitchen floor and fell onto his butt.

My father called out to Hiroshi-san for a small order of ika and wasabi. He told him it was the last dish of the night as he was getting full and would like to share it with my mom. Hiroshi-san nodded with a forced smile and prepared the ika dish right at the sushi bar quite quickly when he realized he was out of wasabi by the bar. He went back into the kitchen only to find Junichi-san sitting on the kitchen floor, rubbing his back. Hiroshi-san ignored him, grabbed the wasabi paste from the shelf by the remaining sake bottles, adjusted the remaining sake bottles so they too would not fall, and then shook his head as he exited the kitchen, not once addressing Junichi-san.

Zen Wasabi hides in the shadows of the narrow pyloric cecum as several saketroopers waddles past him in the main pyloric duct. He checks to make sure they're gone, then runs down the main pyloric duct in the opposite direction. Squid Vader appears at the far end of the main pyloric duct and starts after the old Red-Eye.

My father adjusted the dishes in front of him to make room for the ika. He moved the karei dish, miso bowl and the soy sauce bottle more towards the sushi bar ice box, away from him. He poured another sake for his neighbor and then himself and placed the sake bottle on his right side, nearest the neighbor. The neighbor bowed his thanks to my father with blurry, red eyes.

Soy-3PO looks around at the saketroopers milling about the Millennium Flounder entry ramp in the docking bay. Miso-D2, with a strand of seaweed lodged into the Death Starfish's brain, turns his top bowl left and right, burping a response. Prawn Solo and Unagibacca hussle down a long pyloric duct with several saketroopers hot on their tail.

A saketrooper yells out to another, "Close the blast pores!"

At the end of the main pyloric duct, blast pores begin to close in front of them. The shellfish starfish pilot and his saucy companion ooze past the huge pores just as they are closing, and manage to get off a couple of laserbean blasts at the pursuing saketroopers before the pores slam shut.

The same saketrooper screams out, "Open the blast pores! Open the blast pores!"

Hiroshi-san then delivered 2 pieces of ika sushi, squid on rice, on a small white serving dish with a glob of wasabi on the side to my father. My father poured a little more soy sauce into his soy sauce dish and rubbed his hands together after a deep breath. He thanked Hiroshi-san and Hiroshi-san bowed. My father grabbed his chopsticks. My mother sighed, stated she was very full, but resigned and grabbed her chopsticks as well.

Obi-Wan Wasabi hurries along one of the pyloric ducts leading to the docking bay where the Millennium Flounder waits. Just before he reaches the hangar, Squid Vader lurches into view at the end of the main pyloric duct, not ten centimeters away. Squid Vader lights his chopsabers. Obi-Wan Wasabi also ignites his chopsabers and globs slowly forward.

Squid Vader says, "I've been waiting for you, Obi-Wan Wasabi. We meet again, at last. The kaiten-zushi, sushi on the conveyor belt, has now completed it's final lap."

Obi-Wan Wasabi moves with elegant ease into a classical offensive position. The fearsome Dark Lord of the Surf takes a definsive stance, tentacles waving about in an intimidating manner.

Squid Vader continues, "When I left you, I was the apprentice, a mere shoaling squid. Now, I am the master."

Obi-Wan Wasabi retorts, "Only a master of evil, Squid. Your true ink shows." The two masters square off.

My father grabbed the first piece of ika sushi with his chopsticks and then led it the soy sauce only to stop abruptly. He looked at my mom and apologized as he offered the ika still in his chopsticks to my mom. He moved it about encouraging her to simply take it out of his chopsticks with her chopsticks. As my mother approached the ika sushi with her own chopsticks, Hiroshi-san ran over to my father, waving his hands, saying, "No! No! No! Tom-san! Sorry, no!"

My father stopped moving, wondering what was so serious that prompted Hiroshi-san to be so forward and vocal. He looked around him to see if something was wrong happening around him in the restaurant. He saw nothing out of the ordinary in that split second. Hiroshi-san gently placed his hand on my mother's hand that held the chopsticks and lowered her hand for her. She let him. My father looked at Hiroshi-san with a very perplexed look.

Hiroshi-san calmly said, "Tom-san, I am so very sorry, but you cannot place two pairs of chopsticks on the same food item. It is a very serious social offense for Japanese people."

My father was surprised by this. He explained to Hiroshi-san that he had traveled in Japan quite a bit and that he never heard of such a thing. Of course, he also explained that it had never come up. Then my father asked Hiroshi-san why this was so offensive in Japan. Hiroshi-san said, "Quite frankly Tom-san, it reminds all Japanese of a funeral of a loved one. When the body of a loved one is cremated, it is our history and custom that the remaining family picks the deceased's bones from the ashes with large chopsticks and for the large bones, it requires two people to pick the bone at the same time. This is the only time two sets of chopsticks may be on the same item. It is a very sad but respectful ceremony. So, place the ika sushi onto Linda-san's dish, please. Please do not put two chopsticks together on the same item. Please. Please."

My father nodded with a horrified yet apologetic look on his face. He seemed to have lost his appetite. He recovered a bit and then apologized to Hiroshi-san and then to his neighbor by bowing. Hiroshi-san simply said, "Thank you. So sorry. Thank you."

The two galaxsean warriors sit perfectly still for a few moments, sizing each other up and waiting for the right moment. Obi-Wan Wasabi seems to be under increasing pressure and strain, as if an invisible grater were being placed upon him. He shakes his glob and, blinking, tries to clear his red eyes. Obi-Wan Wasabi makes a sudden lunge at the huge warrior but is checked by a lightning fast movement from the Dark Lord of The Surf. A masterful slash stroke by Squid Vader is blocked by the old Red-Eye. Another of the Red-Eye's blows is blocked, then countered. Wasabi moves around the Dark Lord of the Surf and starts backing into the massive spacefish hangar. The two powerful warriors sit motionless for a few moments with chopsabers locked in mid-air, creating a high-pitched clicking sound. Click, click, click... click, click, click.

Squid Vader says, "Your powers are weak, old root."

Obi-Wan Wasabi responds, "You can't win, Squid. If you chop me down, I shall become more powerful than you can possibly imagine, providing good taste throughout the oceanverse."

Their chopsabers continue to meet in combat, clicking about. Clickety, click, click, click. Click. Click.

Junichi-san had fully recovered from his fall in the kitchen. He started arranging dishes by the sink to be washed. He loaded some dishes into the dishwasher and then looked at the starfish serving dish and shook his head. He clearly had no easy way to clean this type of dish. It didn't fit into the dishwasher so he would eventually have to wash this one by hand.

Instead of washing the starfish serving dish, he left the kitchen and came around to collect more dishes. He collected the karei dish in front of my father and bowed for his approval. My father nodded his thanks. He returned to the kitchen and placed the karei dish, that still had some flounder bits on it, by the starfish serving dish.

Prawn Solo and Unagibacca, their weapons drawn, lean back against the wall surveying the forward bay, watching the Imperial saketroopers make their rounds of the hangar.

Prawn asks Unagibacca, "Didn't we just leave this party?"

Unagibacca growls a reply as Luke Soywalker and Princess Maki join them. Prawn asks, "What kept you?"

Princess Maki smarts back, "We ran into some old friends."

Luke asks, "Is the spacefish alright?"

Prawn answers, "Seems okay, if we can get to it. Just hope that the old root got the tractor bean out of commission."

Squid Vader and Obi-Wan Wasabi continue their powerful duel. As they hit their chopsabers together, ancient glowing wood shards fly about on impact. Saketroopers look on in interest as the old Red-Eye and the Dark Lord of the Surf fight. Suddenly Luke spots the battle from his group's vantage point and calls out, "Look!"

Luke, Princess Maki, Prawn, and Unagibacca look up and see Zen Wasabi and Squid Vader emerging from the main pyloric duct on the far side of the docking bay.

Junichi-san returned to my father's area on the sushi bar and offered to take the soy sauce bottle and miso bowl in front of him away. My father looked at the soy sauce dish by his side, saw plenty in there, and nodded. Junichi-san took them into the kitchen immediately and placed the soy sauce on the shelf by the sake bottles since there was a little more room there now. He placed the miso bowl by the sink, near the starfish serving dish. He looked up at the soy sauce bottle on the shelf and seemed to realize it was not the best place to keep it and brought it down to the counter by the sink.

Soy-3PO and Miso-D2 are in the center of the Death Starfish's Imperial docking bay.

Soy-3PO calls out, "Come on, Miso-D2. We're going!"

The soyd waddles out of sight as the seven saketroopers who were guarding the spacefish roll past them heading towards Obi-Wan Wasabi and the Dark Surf Knight. Soy-3PO continues to encourage Miso-D2 to move forward.

Prawn, Unagibacca, Luke and Princess Maki tensely watch the duel. The saketroopers roll toward the battling knights.

Prawn yells, "Now's our chance! Go!"

After learning about the near disastrous and offensive social faux pas my parents almost committed, my father put the piece of ika sushi on my mother's dish right away. He then used one of his chopsticks to cut the glob of wasabi on the ika serving dish in half. He grabbed the half closest to him and placed it into his soy sauce in the small soy sauce dish and started swirling it about. He then grabbed the last piece of ika and swirled it about in the wasabi-infused sauce.

They start for the Millennium Flounder. Obi-Wan Wasabi sees the saketroopers charging toward him and realizes that he is trapped. Squid Vader takes advantage of Wasabi's momentary distraction and brings his mighty chopsaber down on the old glob of root. Obi-Wan manages to deflect the blow and swiftly turns around. The old Red-Eye Knight looks over his nori at Luke, lifts his chopsaber from Squid Vader's then watches his opponent with a serene look on his face. Squid Vader brings his chopsaber down, cutting old Zen in half. Zen's nori falls to the floor in two parts, but Zen is not in it. Squid Vader is puzzled at Obi-Wan Wasabi's disappearance and pokes at the empty nori. As the guards are distracted, the sushi adventurers and the roebots reach the spacefish. Luke sees Zen cut in two and starts for him.

Aghast, Luke screams out, "No!"

The saketroopers turn toward Luke and begin firing laserbeans at him. The roebots are already moving up the ramp into the Millennium Flounder, while Luke, transfixed by anger and awe, returns their laserbean fire. Prawn joins in the laserbean firefight. Squid Vader looks up and advances toward them, as one of his saketroopers is struck down, glass shattering, sake pouring out.

Prawn yells at Luke, "Come on!"

Princess Maki calls out as well, "Come on! Luke, it's too late!"

Prawn barks out, "Blast the pore, soy!"

In the kitchen, Junichi-san walked back and forth from the sink to the dishwasher, his feet crunching on some remaining glass pieces of sake bottles that he failed to clean up completely. He threw some shucked edamame husks into the trash compactor on top of the sake bottle shards as he looked at his feet, either ensuring that his feet were not going to be harmed by any remaining shards on the floor.

Luke fires his laserbean pistol at the pore control panel, and it explodes. The pore begins to shut. Three saketroopers roll forward firing laserbean bolts, as the pore slides to a close behind them, shutting Squid Vader and the other saketroopers out of the docking bay. A saketrooper lies dead at the fins of his onrushing compatriots. Luke starts for the advancing saketroopers, as Prawn Solo and Princess Maki move up the ramp into the spacefish. He fires, hitting a saketrooper, who shatters onto the floor.

Obi-Wan Wasabi's voice is heard by Luke saying, "Run gelatinously, Luke! Run gelatinously!"

Luke looks around to see where the voice came from. He turns toward the spacefish, ducking Imperial laserbean fire from the saketroopers and runs gelatinously into the spacefish.

Junichi-san grabbed the water sprayer out of the sink before him and then grabbed the karei dish. He looked into the arms of the starfish serving dish, grimaced at all the food remnants inside, and then power washed the karei dish clear. He put the dish to the side of the sink after all of the food remnants were gone. Then he placed the starfish serving dish into the left side of the industrial sink. It didn't fit very well. It was so large, two of the arms stuck way above the edge of the sink. He sprayed the inside of each arm with the water sprayer and cleared out all of the food remnants. After getting through all of the other dishes near the sink, he carried them over to the dishwasher and entered them all in very neatly. He placed the karei dish from my father's place setting in last, closed the dishwasher door, and hit a few buttons. Dishwasher noises started almost immediately.

Prawn Solo pulls back on the nerve controls of the Millennium Flounder and the spacefish begins to move. The dull thuds of laserbean bolts bouncing off the outside skin of the spacefish are heard and felt as Unagibacca adjusts the nerve controls before him in the fishhead.

Prawn nervously says, "I hope the old root got that tractor bean out of commission or this is going to be a real short trip. Okay, hit it!"

Unagibacca growls in agreement.

The Millennium Flounder powers away from the Death Starfish docking bay, makes a spectacular turn and disappears into the vastness of the oceanverse. Success.

9 GAI FIGHTERS

After a long evening, we finished our food. I finally got around to eating my kushi and it was quite good. My father talked a lot tonight to his neighbor and my mother seemed very relaxed near the end of the meal. My father didn't drink as much as he usually did so I think mom thought this would be an easier journey home than usual.

My father called over to Hiroshi-san and asked for the check. Junichi-san came around and started clearing all of the dishes in front of us. He asked if we wanted to take home the leftovers and my mother nodded with a smile.

I was very tired. I tried to hold back my yawns though because every time I yawn, my mom thinks I need to go to bed earlier.

Hiroshi-san brought the check over but my father kept talking with our neighbor. Our neighbor also asked for his check. As I looked around, I realized we and our neighbor were, again, the last customers in the restaurant. Hiroshi-san gathered and organized the leftover fish from the day. There wasn't much as it had been a pretty busy day. I saw him pack up some shrimp from the bar's ice bin into a container. He took out some sliced eel fillet and packaged that in clear wrap. Junichi-san returned with some of our rolls and tofu in a to-go container. He placed that in a bag with some soy sauce packets. Hiroshi-san then asked if we wanted some miso soup to go for home as he had a lot left over. My mother smiled graciously and thanked him. He prepared the soup in a to-go plastic container with a strong lid.

Just as they placed our to-go packages on the bar next to the leftovers headed for the refrigerator, the back door delivery bell rang. Hiroshi-san looked very confused and said something in Japanese to Junichi-san as he looked at the clock on the wall. Junichi-san entered the kitchen and answered the door cautiously. A few seconds later, he emerged whispering something in Hiroshi-san's ear. They both looked concerned and proceeded to go to the kitchen, leaving their leftovers and our to-go items on the bar, which I found unusual. I quickly dismissed this though as I saw all of the leftovers sitting on the bar in their various containers. My imagination took over.

In the central stomach area of the Millennium Flounder, Luke, saddened by the loss of Obi-Wan Wasabi, stares off blankly as the roebots look on. Princess Maki puts a nori around him protectively, and Luke turns and looks up at her. She sits down beside him.

Back in the fishhead of the Millennium Flounder, Prawn Solo spots approaching enemy spacefish.

He calls out to Unagibacca, "We're coming up on the sentry spacefish. Hold 'em off! Angle the deflector shells while I cook up the main laserbeans!"

Back in the stomach hold, Luke looks downward sadly, shaking his head back and forth, as Princess Maki smiles comfortingly at him.

Luke mourns, "I can't believe he's gone."

Miso-D2 burps a sad reply.

Maki comforts, "There wasn't anything you could have done. He roots for us now."

Suddenly, Prawn Solo rushes into the stomach hold area where Luke is sitting with the princess and calls out to Luke, "C'mon soy buddy! We're not out of this yet!"

My father sensed a bit of concern from Hiroshi-san and Junichi-san before they went into the kitchen. When they didn't return right away, he stood up from the sushi bar and peered into the kitchen but his view was obstructed by the noren curtains. We all knew it was odd that there would be a delivery at closing time. My father called out, "Hiroshi-san? Hiroshi-san! Is everything ok?" I heard some discussion back in the kitchen but couldn't make out the words. I peered into the kitchen by leaning over the sushi bar and saw Hiroshi-san and Junichi-san talking with someone wearing a black hat. They were very animated and seemed stressed. Seconds later, Hiroshi-san quickly emerged from the kitchen responding to my father's call. When the curtains flew apart in Hiroshi-san's wake, I got a clear look at the man talking to Junichi-san. It was the tall, dark man from earlier in the evening!

Hiroshi-san looked very worried and glanced back at the kitchen as he approached my father. In a low voice, he told my father, "Uh... Tom-san, not sure what is going on but delivery is not from normal delivery man so I must handle this right away. So sorry. Just a few minutes. Ok?" My father nodded with a concerned look on his face and asked Hiroshi-san if he needed help. Hiroshi-san politely and calmly declined.

I looked at my father, raised an eyebrow and signaled to him that I was going to use the restroom. He nodded. I wanted to go to the restroom because I knew I could eavesdrop on the kitchen conversation. I think my father also recognized that and figured I would be able to tell him what was going on in there.

I entered the restroom and put my ear to the wall shared by the restroom and kitchen. There were no dishwashers, hand dryers or other machines running, so it was relatively easy to hear the conversation. I heard Hiroshi-san speak first.

Hiroshi-san said, "No, sir. I will not be intimidated by you or by your employer."

The tall, dark man spoke, "With all due respect, in this day and age, you will need to realize that you may not be in a position to take that stance."

Junichi-san interrupted and was very upset, "Why you deliver clams?! Why you..."

Hiroshi-san must have raised his hand or something to stop Junichi-san, instructed him to leave the kitchen. I assumed he left the kitchen to take care of my dad and our neighbor because he said nothing more after that.

"Regarding the clams," Hiroshi-san continued, "how am I to know these are not tampered with?"

"You do not know. I will tell you that they are not but why should you believe me? That is the point, is it not? I am demonstrating to you that I can affect your business in a very real and tangible way should you not consider our..." The man paused dramatically. He continued in a questioning tone, "...generous offer."

Hiroshi-san spoke loudly, out of frustration, "Generous offer?! Offer?! You, sir, disrespect me and my business. What you present here is not an offer. It is an insult and it is hostile! It is trying to destroy all that I have built over many, many years! This is not an offer! And it certainly is not anything I will even consider!! Now, sir, please leave!! We have customers."

The tall, dark man laughed mildly and said, "This will not be the easiest path for you Mr. Moto Sushi. My employer will not be pleased, which means I will not be pleased, and, in turn, that means, you, sir, will not be pleased." He laughed again.

Hiroshi-san simply replied, "Do not threaten me! Now go. Go now."

I heard the back door slam shut so I left the restroom to return to the sushi bar. My father was gathering all of our leftovers and was getting ready to leave. Apparently, Junichi-san must have said something to him to curb his concerns. Hiroshi-san emerged from the kitchen carrying a box of seemingly fresh clams on ice and handed the heavy box to Junichi-san. As he did so, he instructed him to do something with it in

Japanese. My father asked, "Everything ok? Ready to go?" I was concerned but nodded just the same. I wasn't really sure what exactly I heard in the restroom but telling my dad on the way home was probably the best thing to do. It seemed serious though.

Junichi-san lifted the heavy box of clams onto the sushi bar and tripped. The box launched out of his hands and spilled across the sushi bar. Clams and ice broke out of the ripped box and flew everywhere hitting our leftovers and bouncing off and around the bar.

Prawn Solo climbs into his attack position in the topside gunfin eye turret of the Millennium Flounder. Likewise, Luke Soywalker gets up and moves out toward the gunfins as Princess Maki heads for the fishhead to see what is going on. Luke climbs down the bones into the other gunfin, settling in front of one of the two main laserbean cannons mounted in a large rotating eye turret on the topside of the spacefish. Prawn fits on an antennae headset as he sits before the nerves of his laserbean cannon, then speaks into the antenna and says, "You in, soy? Okay, stay gelatinous!"

Unagibacca and Princess Maki search the nearby oceanverse for attacking Gai Fighters. The Wookieel pulls back on the speed nerves as the Millennium Flounder bounces slightly. Brain readouts form on Prawn Solo's target membrane on the eye lens in front of him as he reaches for the controls. Luke sits in readiness for the attack, his soy on the laserbean cannon's controls. Unagibacca spots the enemy spacefish and squeals.

Princess Maki gets on the conuslink and yells, "Here they come!"

The Imperial Gai Fighters move towards the Millennium Flounder, one each veering off to the left and right of the pirate spacefish. The platters whip past behind the Imperial pilot as he adjusts his fineuvering hydro-stick. The Gai Fighter races past the Millennium Flounder, firing laserbeans as it passes. Soy-3PO is seated in the stomach hold area, next to Miso-D2. The pirate spacefish bounces and vibrates as the nervous system goes out in the stomach area and then comes back on. A Gai Fighter fineuvers in front of Prawn Solo, who follows it and fires at it with the laserbean cannon. Luke does likewise, as the Gai Fighter streaks into view. The spacefish has suffered a minor hit and bounces slightly. Two Gai Fighters dive down toward the pirate spacefish. Luke fires at a passing Gai Fighter.

He exclaims, "They're coming in too fast!"

The Gai Fighters charge and laserbeans streak from all of the spacefish. The Millennium Flounder spacefish shudders as a laserbean hits very close to the fishhead. The Wookieel chatters something to Princess Maki. Another Gai Fighter soars across firing on the pirate spacefish. Two Gai Fighters fire a barrage of laserbeans at the

Millennium Flounder. A laserbean streaks into the side of the spacefish as it lurches violently, throwing poor Soy-3PO into an air sac full of brain data seeds. Princess Maki watches the brain readout on the panel membrane as Unagibacca finipulates the spacefish's nerve controls.

Princess Maki informs the crew, "We've lost lateral and pectoral controls."

Prawn Solo retorts, "Don't worry, she'll hold together."

An enemy laserbean hits the spacefish's nerve panel, causing it to blow out in a shower of fiery bean fragments.

Prawn Solo talks quietly to the Millennium Flounder, "You hear me, fish egg? Hold together!"

Miso-D2 advances toward the steaming bean nerve panel, removing the steam by spraying it with cold soy milk, burping and bubbling all the while.

Luke swivels in his gun mount, following the Gai Fighter with his laserbean cannon. Prawn Solo aims his laserbean cannon at the enemy as well. A Gai Fighter streaks in front of the Millennium Flounder as Princess Maki watches it soar over the spacefish. Another Gai Fighter heads right for the pirate spacefish and then zooms by overhead. Luke follows the Gai Fighter across his field of view, firing laserbeans from his cannon. A Gai Fighter dives past the spacefish. Luke fires at a Gai Fighter. At his fin eye turret, Prawn follows a Gai Fighter in his sights and releases a blast of laserbeans. He connects and the Gai Fighter explodes into gooey, soy-bean-encrusted shell dust. He laughs victoriously. Two other Gai Fighters move toward and over the Millennium Flounder and unleash a barrage of laserbeans at the spacefish. Another Gai Fighter moves in on the pirate spacefish and Luke, smiling, fires the laserbean cannon at it, scoring a spectacular direct hit.

Luke exclaims, "Got him! I got him!"

Prawn Solo turns and gives Luke a victory wave which Luke soyfully returns by waving a mass of atsuage. He says, "Great, soy! Don't get saucy!" Prawn returns to his laserbean cannon as two more Gai Fighters cross in front of the spacefish.

While Unagibacca finipulates the controls, Princess Maki turns and looks over her nori out the fishhead and says, "There are still two more of those Gais out there!"

A Gai Fighter moves up over the spacefish, firing laserbeans at it. Luke and Prawn look into their respective brain readout target membranes. An Imperial Gai Fighter crosses Prawn's gunfin turret and he swivels in his chair, following it with blasts from his laserbean cannon. Another Gai Fighter crosses Luke's gunfin and he reacts in a like manner with the glow of his target brain readout membrane lighting his soyish face.

The Gai Fighter zooms toward the Millennium Flounder, firing destructive blasts at it. Luke fires a laserbean blast at the approaching enemy Gai Fighter and it bursts into a spectacular shell explosion. Luke's brain readout target membrane records the hit. The pirate spacefish bounces slightly as it is struck by enemy fire. The last of the attacking Imperial Gai Fighters looms in and fires again upon the Millennium Flounder.

Prawn Solo swivels behind his cannon with his aim following the arc of the Gai Fighter. The Gai Fighter comes closer, firing at the pirate spacefish, but a well-aimed blast from Prawn Solo's laserbean cannon hits the attacker. The Gai Fighter blows up in a small atomic shower of steaming shell fragments.

Luke laughs, "That's it! We did it!"

Princess Maki rolls up and gives Unagibacca a congratulatory nudge and yells, "We did it!"

My father jumped up once the clams and ice cubes bounced about, tried to catch the ones headed for him, and was trying to somehow otherwise help Junichi-san from too much embarrassment. Once the clams and ice settled, my dad brushed them off of the leftover containers and placed them carefully on the other side of the bar for Junichi-san to clean up. They covered the bar. A bottle of soy sauce was toppled and was leaking onto the bar. My father picked it up.

Soy-3PO lies on the floor of the spacefish, completely tangled in the steaming, sparking nerves of the Millennium Flounder. He cries for help, "Help! I think my glass is melting!" He looks over to Miso-D2 and says, "This is all your fault."

Miso-D2 turns his bowl from side to side and gurgles in response. Steam oozes out from under his top bowl.

The victorious Millennium Flounder swims off majestically through the oceanverse.

As my father and the neighboring customer continued to help Junichi-san clean up the clams and ice, I happened to glance out the front window only to see the tall, dark man walking by. Without thinking, I quickly ran to the front door of Moto Sushi, slightly opened it and peered out toward the direction that the tall, dark man was walking. He met up with someone in a long trench coat and started talking.

I couldn't hear much of the conversation with the noise of the city in the background but I heard "Are you sure?" and then "box of clams" and then something that sounded like "quite some risk". I really couldn't make much sense of it though.

I didn't want to risk being spotted so I slid back inside the restaurant. My father was right in front of me when I turned around, ready to leave. He smiled at me, asked if everything was alright and patted me on the head. I told him, "I'm a little confused and a little worried about Hiroshi-san and his place. I heard some things in the bathroom." He told me to tell him on the subway ride home because it was getting late. My mom agreed. We waved to Hiroshi-san and Junichi-san and headed outside. The tall, dark man and the man in the trench coat were gone.

Back in the Death Starfish, Squid Vader oozes into the control center where Grand Moff Tarako is watching the huge brain readout membrane with a galaxsea of platters before him. Tarako asks, "Are they away?"

Squid Vader replies, "They have just made the jump into hypersea." Tarako looks skeptically at Squid Vader and says, "You're sure the homing beancon is secure aboard their spacefish? I'm taking an awful risk, Vader. This had better work."

My father handed me the clear leftover boxes that held the shrimp, rolls and tofu to carry. On the subway ride home, I told my father what I thought I had heard both in the bathroom and when I leaned outside the door of the restaurant. He simply raised his eyebrows at it all and thought for a while. He said, "Well, son... I'm not sure what you heard but it seemed like Hiroshi-san had everything under control. I wouldn't worry too much about it." I told him it seemed like Hiroshi-san was mad or worried or something like that. My mother said that we could ask them how it was all going next week on our next visit. I think she was appeasing me at that moment and was hoping I would forget all about it by the time we came back to Moto Sushi. I was really concerned. I wouldn't forget. My parents didn't seem to want to really get involved.

That was the end of the conversation. So, I sat there on the subway seats, hiding yawns from my parents, and stared into the to-go boxes. I looked at the rolls and at the shrimp all the way to our home stop.

Prawn Solo removes his fin-protectors and smiles as he sits at the fishhead nerve controls of the Millennium Flounder. Unagibacca moves into the aft section to check the damage to the spacefish. Princess Maki is near Prawn.

Prawn looks at Princess Maki and says, "Not a bad bit of rescuing, huh? You know, sometimes I even amaze myshellf."

Princess Maki retorts, "That doesn't sound too hard. Besides, they let us go. It's the only explanation for the ease of our escape."

Prawn looks shocked and replies, "Easy?! You call that easy?"
Princess Maki says, "They're tracking us!"
"Not this spacefish, sister."
A frustrated Princess Maki, shakes her rolls and says, "At least the information in Miso-D2 is still intact."
Prawn asks, "What's so important? What's he carrying? Let me guess, a secret soup recipe, right?"
She replies, "The technical readouts of that Death Starfish Station. I only hope that when the data is analyzed, a weakness can be found. It's not over yet!"
Prawn laughs, "It is for me, sister! Look, I ain't in this for your revolution, and I'm not in it for you, Princess. I expect to be well paid. I'm in it for the cowry shells!"
"You needn't worry about your reward. If cowry shells are all that you love, then that's what you'll receive!"
Princess Maki angrily turns and starts out of the fishhead, passing Luke coming in, on her way out.
She looks at him and says, "Your friend is quite a mercenary, a piranha of sorts. I wonder if he really cares about anything... or anyone."
Luke says, "I care!"
Luke, shaking his gelatinous head, sits in the co-pilot seat of the fishhead. He and Prawn stare out at the vast oceanverse before them.
Luke asks, "So, what do you think of her, Prawn?"
Prawn replies, "I'm not trying to, soy!"
Luke, under his breath, utters, "Good."
Prawns says, "Still she's got a lot of spirit. I don't know, what do you think? Do you think a princess and a shrimp like me..."
Luke interrupts, "No!"
Luke looks away. Prawn smiles at young Luke Soywalker's jealousy.

10 THE PLATE YAFIN

The week went by very fast. Between all of my school work, basketball practice, and many attempts at video game domination, I found myself right back on the subway Friday evening, heading to Moto Sushi. On the ride there, I realized I hadn't thought much about Moto Sushi all week, as my mother was hoping, and started wondering how Hiroshi-san and the tall, dark man situation was going. As I thought more about it, I had wondered if there was anything really to worry about or if my imagination was running wild. I had thought I had heard the tall, dark man threaten Hiroshi-san when I was in the restroom but perhaps I was just turning it into something dramatic when it was likely just normal business. Maybe I had watched too many movies.

I asked my dad about the events of last week at Moto Sushi on the way there. He shrugged his shoulders and said that Hiroshi-san was a keen business man and that if there were issues with his business, he would handle them. His dedication to sushi and the restaurant was obvious and even though I still didn't care to eat sushi, it was clear that he cared about it so much that he devoted his life to making Moto Sushi the best it could be... or so my parents said.

We arrived at Moto Sushi a bit earlier than usual. My father didn't work as late as he had been for the past several weeks. We walked into the restaurant and it was very quiet. In fact, there were no customers at all. It was early for dinner, but I was surprised to see an empty sushi bar. Not even Hiroshi-san or Junichi-san were about. My parents were surprised by this too. My mother called out, "Hiroshi-san! Hiroshi-san?"

Hiroshi-san emerged from the kitchen, looking rather disheveled, like he had experienced a rough day already.

"Yes. Yes, I am here Mrs. McKay," he said hurriedly.

My mother asked, "Is everything ok? Are we too early for dinner?"

125

"Uh... no, no, no. Of course not. Ah... everything ok. Just very busy day. Please... please, sit down."

My mother looked around and then ushered my father and me to our usual place by the bar. There were no table settings at the bar, which was very unusual. Every other time before, there were place settings with a small serving dish, a soy sauce dish, a moist towelette, napkin, a water glass, and chopsticks. This evening there was nothing other than the usual soy sauce bottles scattered about along the back of the bar. As we sat down, Junichi-san came out of the kitchen with dishes and hurriedly started constructing our place settings. Junichi-san apologetically nodded as he placed a new red serving dish in the shape of a fish's fin and a green soy sauce dish in front of each of us. He said in his heavy accent, "Uh... new dishes now for eating and soy. Nice, I think. Like fish fin and green this one like wasabi, no? Ha ha." He chuckled nervously and bowed as he returned to the kitchen. I began to wonder if the reason the table settings were not set up yet was due to them having new dishes. Did the old ones break? Just time to refresh things? I didn't really know but things felt odd around here this time.

Hiroshi-san explained they were running a bit late and that the setup for today was unexpectedly long. They had some trouble getting some of their daily fish shipments, but it had all worked out and the fish had arrived eventually and was indeed fresh. Also, in that same day, he told us he had to get new dishes, but he didn't really explain why. He just said they were all broken. He quickly changed the subject and asked for our first course order right away and my mother ordered some miso soup, some karei, or flounder, a sampler plate containing 2 pieces of shrimp sushi, 2 California rolls, 2 unagi, some pollack roe, some atsuage soy, and a side of edamame. Hiroshi-san looked over at me after taking my mom's order and I said, "Kushi, please."

He simply nodded.

This was the first time Hiroshi-san hadn't tried to convince me to try sushi or sashimi. Something was definitely wrong. He couldn't have possibly given up on his quest to get me to like, or even try, sushi. I was getting more concerned.

My father then asked Hiroshi-san about any specials he might have available. Hiroshi-san said there were a couple today including Amakusa starfish, a special starfish from an island off the coast of Japan. My father then said, "Well, surprise me. I'm feeling adventurous! Although I'm not sure about the starfish. That didn't go well last time." Hiroshi-san nodded, smiled very quickly, and then made his way to the kitchen.

When the sushi arrived, my imagination took over... especially, with these new red fin dishes and green dishes in play! Junichi-san returned from the kitchen carrying a bulky box containing a large amount of seaweed sheets. He took out a ream of nori and placed it on the preparation area of the bar for making sushi. He then took out Hiroshi-san's very old wooden block of knives from beneath the counter and placed them by the seaweed sheets. He took out each knife, inspected the blades and handles, and returned them to the block with a nod. He then proceeded to the refrigerator and started inventorying the fish for the night.

Hiroshi-san began to prepare the sushi mom ordered. First to arrive in front of my mom was the karei, then the sampler plate, and the bowl of edamame. Junichi-san then brought over miso soup for each of us. Hiroshi-san informed us that he had some very fresh grouper and scad as well as some tobiuo, or flying fish, if we were interested. The scad was a special Rainbow Runner scad from Japan and was not yet prepared but available with a little preparation time. It was a unique fish for sushi, but quite expensive. My mother simply nodded and smiled said, "Hmmm... I guess we should have a small order of that as well." Hiroshi-san smiled, nodded and started to prepare 2 pieces of Rainbow Runner sashimi. My father smiled, looked at my mother, and said, "That must be the real special!"

The Millennium Flounder drifts into orbit around the plate Yafin and proceeds to one of its orbiting tiny, green soy dishes, a saucer called Massassea. The spacefish floats over the dense jungle of seaweed on Massassea. An alert guard, his laserbean gun in fin, scans the vast seaweedscape before him. He sets the laserbean gun down and looks toward an ancient block, barely visible through the seaweed foliage.

Rotting in a reef of seaweed, the ancient Temple of Knife Block lies shrouded in an eerie mist. The air is heavy with the fantastic cries of unimaginable fish. Prawn Solo, Luke Soywalker, and the others are greeted by the Rebel Groupers. Luke and the group ride on an armored military Rainbow Runner and glide into the massive knife block temple through an empty knife slot.

The Rainbow Runner stops in a huge spacefish hangar, set up in the interior of the heavily worn knife block. Gillard, the Clammander of the Rebel forces, rushes up to the group and gives Princess Maki a big, awkward hug with his shell. Everyone is pleased to see her.

Gillard continues to hold Princess Maki and joyfully says, "You're safe! You haven't unrolled! We had feared the worst." Gillard composes himself, slides back and bows formally. He continues, "When we heard about Abaloneraan, we were afraid that you were... lost along with your father."

Princess Maki responds, "We don't have time for our sorrows, Clammander. The Death Starfish has surely tracked us here." She looks pointedly at Prawn Solo and continues, "It's the only explanation for the ease of our escape. You must use the dataseeds in this Miso-D2 unit to plan the attack. It is our only hope."

Just as mom placed her first piece of sushi on her plate, the door to Moto Sushi opened. The tall, dark man glided through the door, paused to look around the restaurant for just a few seconds and smiled at the emptiness he saw. He then approached the bar, wearing a long, dark coat. I sat there staring at him, jaw opened, but my parents barely noticed that the man had entered.

The surface of the Death Starfish ominously approaches the red plate, Yafin. Inside the Death Starfish control room, Grand Moff Tarako and Squid Vader, Lord of the Surf, are interrupted in their discussion by the buzz of the conuslink. Tarako moves to answer the call. The voice on the other side of the conuslink states, "We are approaching the plate, Yafin. The Rebel secret plate is on a saucer on the far side. We are preparing to orbit the plate."

I whispered across my mom's place setting at my dad, "Dad, Dad, Dad!" When I was finally able to grab his attention, he leaned in and said, "What's going on, son?" As he said this, he turned his head now fully aware of the tall, dark man standing very closely to his right. My father looked up at him and was a little taken aback by how close the man stood to him, considering the rest of the restaurant was empty. I think at that point, it is safe to say my father recognized the man.

The man ignored my father. He didn't acknowledge him in any discernible way. I looked at the tall, dark man and saw him staring directly at Hiroshi-san. I looked at Hiroshi-san and saw him completely frozen, staring back at the tall, dark man. Hiroshi-san put his knife down, placed both hands on the counter, and looked over at my family, then back at the man.

The man rolled up his sleeve, revealing his starfish tattoo on his forearm, and then took an envelope out of his coat's inner pocket and handed it to Hiroshi-san. Hiroshi-san looked at my family again. We said nothing. Hiroshi-san took the envelope hesitantly and then waved it at the man in the direction of the door as if to shoo him out of the restaurant like a pest.

The tall, dark man looked at his tattoo, then back at Hiroshi-san. He rolled his sleeve back down slowly. No words were said the entire time. The man smiled evilly, looked at our family as the evil eroded from his face, tipped his hat, and left the restaurant.

Hiroshi-san looked backed at Junichi-san and shook his head as he bowed. Junichi-san looked at his feet momentarily and then resumed preparing the nori sheets for the evening's customers. As he was packing the nori sheets into a bin by the bar, he glanced around the restaurant with a watchful eye. Hiroshi-san then told Junichi-san to write out the specials for the evening on the chalkboard on the wall by the kitchen and to be sure to include the tobiuo, tobiko, scad and Amakusa starfish. Hiroshi-san called out to him to make sure he added udon noodles as well to the special menu. Hiroshi-san then explained that he got a special shipment of fish in from his cousin in Japan. This seemed unusual. Junichi-san bowed toward Hiroshi-san, filled the chalkboard with specials, and went back into the kitchen. On his way in, he nodded at me and uttered, "Kushi on way."

A lone Rebel guard stands high above the Yafin landscape, surveying the vast seaweed reef. A steamy mist hangs over the jungle of twisted green seaweed. Udondonna, a strong Rebel leader who really uses his noodle, stands before a large chalkboard of specials. Princess Maki and several other seanators are to one side of the giant chalkboard. The low-ceilinged room is filled with spacefish pilots, navigators, and a sprinkling of hydro-soyd roebots. Everyone is listening intently to what Udondonna is saying. Prawn Solo and Unagibacca are standing near the back.

My father looked at Hiroshi-san and asked him if anything was wrong. Hiroshi-san turned back to my dad and quickly threw a fake smile at us. Hiroshi-san said, "Uh, no. It's all ok." He looked down at the thick envelope in his hand. My dad clearly didn't buy it. My mom chimed in and asked, "Hiroshi-san, that man... the one that gave you that envelope, he seems to come by a lot lately and you do not seem happy to see him. Is there an issue with him?"

Hiroshi-san let his shoulders sink and said, "It is of no concern for you. It shall pass." He smiled hopefully. My parents nodded and didn't further pursue the conversation. My father continued to have a concerned look and glanced at me as he raised his shoulders.

Seconds later, Junichi-san poked his head out from between the noren curtains and cried out to Hiroshi-san, "Kasai! Kasai!" Hiroshi-san looked astonished and ran toward the kitchen. He dropped the thick envelope on the bar right in front of me and quickly entered the kitchen.

I looked around and saw my parents looking into the kitchen to see what was happening. The suspense of the tall, dark man and his evil looks got the better me. Something was wrong here. I acted completely on impulse and didn't think about what I did next. I grabbed the envelope off of the bar and looked around again. No one saw me grab it. I asked to be excused to the restroom and my distracted mom glanced my way and hurriedly nodded. I could've asked for anything at that time and gotten an approval just to stop distracting her from her observation of whatever was happening in the kitchen. I quickly ran into the restroom with the envelope. I started sweating. This was probably a bad idea.

There was no turning back now. I closed the door to the restroom, looked at the envelope and saw it was not sealed. I open the envelope cautiously, being sure not to rip anything, and pulled out a letter. The letter was addressed to "the proprietor of Moto Sushi". It looked like a business letter, really formal. I quickly scanned the first sentence and it read, "This letter is to formally state the intention of Dar King Sushi Corporation regarding the purchase of Moto Sushi LLC and associated assets for a total sum of $250,000." I was completely shocked and could not believe what I was reading. I continued quickly and nervously. I read, "This offer is valid for one week from delivery of this notification." Hiroshi-san couldn't sell Moto Sushi. It was his life.

I quickly folded the letter back into the envelope as neatly as I could and ran back out of the restroom. My parents were at the edge of the sushi bar looking into the kitchen through the noren curtains. I didn't know what they were looking at but took the opportunity to return the envelope to the sushi bar near where Hiroshi-san had left it. No one saw me replace it.

Then Hiroshi-san emerged from the kitchen followed by a small plume of smoke and said, "Ah, no problem. No problem." He explained that the oil in the pan used for the kushi spilled onto the burners and started a small oil fire on the stove. He also explained how he quickly put it out and there was no damage. He took a deep breath, collected himself, looked around the sushi bar, spotted the envelope and grabbed it quickly as he further discussed the small fire with my father.

At the Rebel secret plate, Udondonna informs, "The Death Starfish battle station is heavily shelled and carries a firepower greater than half the spacefish fleet. It's defenses are designed around a direct large-scale assault. A small one-fish fighter should be able to penetrate the outer defense."

Other customers started to arrive and ordered their first courses. Moto Sushi was starting to return back to normal. Well, it seemed as normal as it could be given that Hiroshi-san was potentially selling the sushi bar. I thought about this more. Every time I had seen the tall, dark man talk with Hiroshi-san over the last few weeks, he did not look pleased. So, perhaps Hiroshi-san was having financial troubles or maybe he was tired of running the restaurant. The biggest problem was that I couldn't really tell dad either because he'd get mad that I took the letter and read it without permission. I had to figure this out on my own. I still hated sushi, but I actually loved going to Moto Sushi now. Selling to Dar King Sushi didn't sound like a good thing and based on Hiroshi-san's reactions, it was fairly clear that he didn't want to sell it to them.

Goma Leader, a rough looking sesame seed covered roll, stands and addresses Udondonna, "Pardon me for asking, sir, but what good are grub fighters going to be against that?"

Udondonna replies, "Well, the Tempura doesn't consider a small one-fish fighter to be any threat, or they'd have a tighter defense. An analysis of the plans provided by Princess Maki has demonstrated a weakness in the Death Starfish battle station."

Miso-D2 stands next to a similar roebot, makes burping sounds, and turns his top bowl from right to left.

Udondonna continues, "The approach will not be easy. You are required to fineuver straight down this ambulacral groove and skim the surface of the Death Starfish to this point, the mouth. The target area is only two centimeters wide. It's a small mouth port, right in the center of the Death Starfish. The mouth leads directly to the gastroreactor, the core of the pyloric stomach. A precise hit will start a chain gastroreaction which should destroy the Death Starfish battle station."

A murmur of disbelief runs through the room.

Udondonna further explains, "Only a precise hit will set up a chain gastroreaction. The mouth is laserbean ray-shelled, so you'll have to use ponzu sauce torpedoes. They're much slipperier and go down easy!"

Luke Soywalker is sitting next to Wedge of Lemontilles, a hotshot, young citrous garnish of a spacefish pilot.

Wedge of Lemontilles speaks out, "That's impossible, even for a fully automated fish brain."

Luke replies, "It's not impossible. I used to pin womp gnats in my Duskyhopper back home. They're not much bigger than two centimeters."

Udondonna encourages the Rebel groupers and says, "Fin your spacefish! And may the Rice be with you!"

The groupers rise and begin to leave.

11 THE BATTLE AT YAFIN

My parents continued eating their first order of sushi. Junichi-san finally brought out my kushi. As we ate, my parents talked with Hiroshi-san in between him serving customers. The evening was relatively uneventful until about a half hour after we started eating when the tall, dark man with the starfish tattoo entered the sushi restaurant again. This time he was accompanied by a very well dressed woman. She was smiling and seemed to be having a good time. They sat at a table off in the corner of the restaurant.

The Death Starfish begins to move around the plate, Yafin, toward the tiny green saucer plate called Massassea. Grand Moff Tarako and Squid Vader watch a large data membrane with interest, as a circle of pulses intertwines around one another on the membrane showing its position in relation to Yafin and the fourth saucer plate, Massassea.

A voice comes on the conuslink and says, "Orbiting the plate at maximum velocity. The saucer with the Rebel secret plate will be in range in thirty seconds."

Squid Vader relishes the moment and states, "This will be a day long remembered. It has seen the end of Wasabi and it will soon see the end of the Rebellion."

My mother called over Hiroshi-san and ordered some more of the sampler plate, some baigai, and an order of udon noodles. Since the sushi bar was in full swing of dinner, it actually did not take very long for Hiroshi-san to get the sampler plate together and serve it to my parents.

My mother thanked him when it arrived and quickly placed a prawn, some atsuage, and a roll onto my plate which sat in front of my miso soup and the soy sauce bottle. Ugh. She then served herself and my father took what was left on the plate.

At the Massassea outpost, Luke Soywalker, Soy-3PO, and Miso-D2 enter the huge spacefish hangar and hurry along a long line of gleaming spacefish fighters. Crawfish rush around loading last-minute armaments and unlocking power food couplings. In an area isolated from this activity, Luke finds Prawn Solo and Unagibacca loading small boxes onto an armored Rainbow Runner.

A voice over the loudspeaker calls out, "All flight grouper, fish your stations. All flight groupers, fish your stations."

Prawn is deliberately ignoring the activity of the spacefish fighter pilot's preparation. Luke is quite saddened at the sight of his friend's departure.

Luke asks Prawn, "So... you got your reward and you're just leaving then?"

Prawn responds, "That's right, yeah! I got some old cowry shell debts I've got to pay off with this stuff. Even if I didn't, you don't think I'd be fool enough to stick around here, do you? Why don't you come with us? You're pretty good in a fight. I could use you."

Luke, getting angry, replies, "Come on! Why don't you take a look around? You know what's about to happen, what they're up against. They could use a good spacefish pilot like you. You're turning your back on them."

Prawn Solo says, "What good's a reward if you ain't around to use it? Besides, attacking that battle station ain't my idea of courage. It's more like a deep fry."

A frustrated Luke replies sarcastically, "Alright. Well, take care of yourself, Prawn. I guess that's what you're best at, isn't it?"

Luke turns and sludges off and Prawn hesitates, then calls to him, "Hey, Luke... uh, may the Rice be with you!"

Luke turns and sees Prawn Solo wink at him. Luke nods a small gesture of recognition and disappointment toward Prawn and slinks away. Prawn turns to Unagibacca who growls at his captain.

Prawn looks at him and says, "What're you looking' at? I know what I'm doing."

My mother then tried to convince me to try some of her udon noodle soup. I said that my miso soup was still warm and would be enough. She said I really ought to just try it. To get her off of that topic, I dipped my spoon into her udon and tried it. It was ok but not something I would ever order myself.

Luke Soywalker, Princess Maki, and Udondonna meet under a huge spacefish fighter.

Princess Maki asks Luke, "What's wrong?"

Luke replies, "Oh, it's Prawn! I don't know, I really thought he'd change his mind but he seems too shellfish."

"He's got to follow his own stream. No one can choose it for him."

Luke says, "I only wish Zen were here."

Hiroshi-san then came over with a small salad. He placed it in front of my father and said, "McKay-san, this salad is quite good. It has tobikko, uh... flying fish roe, in it. Very special. Ok for you?" My father nodded excitedly as he hadn't tried tobikko before. My mother continued to eat her udon but then asked Hiroshi-san if he actually had flying fish sushi since he had the eggs. She said this in jest but Hiroshi-san actually got excited and explained that his cousin in Japan overnighted him some flying fish and that they called it tobiuo.

My mother tried to pronounce it. Hiroshi-san corrected her by saying it again. She tried again. He shook his head and repeated, "tobiuo". My mom just smiled at him and shrugged.

Princess Maki gives Luke a little kiss, turns, and goes off. As Luke heads for his X-Fin spacefish fighter, a deadly flying spacefish, another spacefish pilot rushes up to him and bumps him. It is his old friend, Baigai, from Tidetooine.

Baigai exclaims, "Luke! I don't believe it! How'd you get here? Are you going out with us?!"

Luke calls out, "Baigai! Of course, I'll be up there with you! Listen, have I got some stories to tell..."

Breaded Leader, a rugged, well-arranged pile of bread crumbs perfectly suited for katsu, stacks up behind Luke and Baigai. He may be crumbly but he has the confident smile of a born leader.

Breaded Leader asks, "Are you... Luke Soywalker? Have you been checked out on the X-Fin?"

Baigai steps in and says, "Sir, Luke is the best spacefish pilot in the outer reef territories."

Breaded Leader crusts Luke on the back as they stop in front of his X-Fin fighter and says, "I met your father once when I was just a doughboy, he was a great spacefish pilot. You'll do alright. If you've got half of your father's skill, you'll do better than alright."

Luke responds, "Thank you, sir. I'll try."

Breaded Leader hurries to his own spacefish.

Baigai addresses Luke, "I've got to get aboard. Listen, you'll tell me your stories when we come back. Alright?"

"I told you I'd make it someday, Baigai."

"You did, alright. It's going to be like old times, Luke. We're a couple of shooting starfish that'll never be stopped!"

Luke laughs and agrees. He heads for his X-FIn spacefish. As Luke begins to climb up the scales into his sleek, deadly spacefish. The crayfish chief, who is working on the spacefish, points to little Miso-D2, who is being hoisted into a pouch on the back of the X-Fin fighter.

He says, "This Miso unit of yours seems a bit beat up. Do you want a new one?"

Luke responds, "Not on your life! That little soyd and I have been through a lot together."

Luke looks over to Miso-D2 and asks if he is ok. The crayfish lower Miso-D2 into the X-FIn. Now a part of the exterior skin of the X-Fin spacefish, the little soyd blurps that he is fine. Luke climbs up into the fishhead of his X-Fin spacefish fighter and puts on his helmet. Soy-3PO looks on from the floor of the massive hangar as the crayfish secure his little partner into Luke's X-Fin. It's an emotional-filled moment as Miso-D2 blurps good-bye.

Soy-3PO calls out to Miso-D2 and says, "Hang on tight, Miso-D2. You've got to come back." Miso-D2 gurgles in response. "You wouldn't want my life to get boring, would you?" Miso-D2 blurps his reply once again.

Junichi-san spotted the tall, dark man in the corner as he came out of the kitchen carrying a shark skin grater and a real wasabi root wrapped in plastic wrap. He stopped, looked around the rest of the restaurant and drew a very concerned look on his face. He shuffled over to Hiroshi-san, dropped the wasabi root onto the bar with the shark skin grater and whispered something into Hiroshi-san's ear. Hiroshi-san did not look up but just nodded. Whatever Junichi-san told him, he already knew or had already considered.

The sushi bar was very busy at this point in the evening. There was a lot of activity, lots of loud discussions, and not a lot of time for Junichi-san or Hiroshi-san to do anything but serve the customers. No one had yet approached the tall, dark man's table. I suspect that they were de-prioritized on purpose. I did see Hiroshi-san glance up at the tall, dark man's table but the tall, dark man was not looking toward the bar. He was talking with his lady friend. Hiroshi-san called out the dish he had just made as he placed it in front of a customer sitting near us at the bar.

All final preparations are made for the approaching battle. The hangar is buzzing with the last minute activity as the spacefish pilots and crayfish alike make their final adjustments. The hum of activity is occasionally trespassed by the distorted voice of the loudspeaker issuing clammands. Coupling noodles are disconnected from the spacefish as they are steamed. Fishhead shells roll smoothly into place over each spacefish pilot. A signal grouper, holding red guiding cherries, directs the spacefish. Luke, with a trace of a smile gracing his mouth, peers about through his roe goggles.

All of a sudden, Luke hears Zen Wasabi's voice that says, "Luke, the Rice will be with you."

Luke is confused at the voice and taps his headphone antennae.

The tall, dark man got up from his table, looked around the restaurant, adjusted himself, and headed toward the sushi bar just as a waitress approached his table with water and ordering menus. The lady accepted the menus and started looking at them.

All that can be seen of the fortress on Massassea is a lone guard standing on a small shelf jutting out above the dense seaweed jungle. The muted gruesome crying sounds that naturally permeate this eerie purgatory are overwhelmed by the plopping uproar of ion gills as four silver X-Fin spacefish catapult from the nori sheets in a tight formation and disappear into the morning steam cover.

Princess Maki, Soy-3PO, and a field clammander sit quietly before the giant chalkboard showing the plate Yafin and its four saucer plates. The red dot on the board that represents the Death Starfish moves ever closer to the Yafin tidal zone. A series of green dots appear on the chalkboard around the fourth saucer plate. A clamor of indistinct chatter fills the war kitchen.

Junichi-san looked up from the bar to see the tall, dark man get up from his table. He tapped Hiroshi-san on the shoulder and whispered a warning into his ear as the tall, dark man approached. Hiroshi-san nodded without looking up. The tall, dark man placed his hands on the sushi bar in front of him and stood between my father and a neighboring customer sitting at the bar, creating an awkward spacing at the bar. The customer nearest him glanced at him with hopes that he would move away quickly, but he didn't say anything to him directly. My father shrugged, looked up at the tall, dark man and kept his eye on him. The tall, dark man looked straight ahead at the back of the bar. He smirked evilly, clearly waiting for Hiroshi-san to approach him. He simply waited there, smirking, not caring who was looking at him.

Hiroshi-san clearly knew that the tall, dark man was standing at the bar even though he never looked up from preparing the tobiuo dish for my mother. He continued to slice and focus on the fish so much that it seemed like he was unaware of anything going on around him. A bead of sweat emerged from his forehead. He kept slicing thin sections of fish off of the flying fish fillet. He kept slicing and sliced more off of the fillet than our whole family could possibly eat in one sitting. He placed the completed sushi on a large, red plate in the shape of a fish's fin. Junichi-san looked concerned and went into the kitchen and returned carrying a tray of many pork katsu fillets ready for breading to make kushikatsu. He placed the tray next to the red plate containing the tobiuo. Hiroshi-san took a deep breath and glanced at the tall, dark man at the sushi bar. The man just stared through him to the back of the bar, holding firm his evil smirk. Hiroshi-san kept his eyes on the man, reached for the bread crumbs in a nearby canister and proceeded to accidentally bread the tobiuo, the flying fish sashimi. He was supposed to bread the pork cutlets but was so distracted and concerned about the tall, dark man's presence that he didn't notice his mistake.

In the Rebel secret plate on Massassea, a conuslink voice warns, "Stand-by alert. Death Starfish approaching. Estimated time to firing range, fifteen minutes." The Death Starfish slowly moves behind the massive red surface of the plate Yafin. Light from a distant platter creates an eerie oceanic glow around a huge plate, Yafin, where many X-Fin fighters swim in formation and pull away into the vast oceanverse.

Breaded Leader lowers his visor and adjusts his laserbean sights. Looking to each side at his finmen and calls out, "All X-fins report in." Breaded Ten, one of the Rebel fighters checks in, speaking into his antennae headset, "Breaded Ten standing by."

Baigai checks his fighter's nerve controls, alert and ready for combat and calls in, "Breaded Three standing by."

Another Rebel fighter checks in, "Breaded Seven standing by."

Jek Katsu-kins, another Rebel fighter in the squadron also checked in, "Breaded Six standing by."

Another Rebel fighter calls in, "Breaded Nine standing by."

Wedge the Lemontilles checks in from his X-Fin, "Breaded Two standing by."

Yet another Rebel fighter calls in, "Breaded Eleven standing by."

Luke Soywalker checks his control panels and calls in, "Breaded Five standing by."

Miso-D2, in position outside of the X-Fin fighter spacefish, turns his top bowl from side to side and makes burping sounds.

Breaded Leader calls out, "Lock X-fins in attack position."

The group of X-Fin fighters move in formation toward the Death Starfish, unfolding the fins and locking them in the flying "X" position.

Breaded Leader continues, "We're passing through their biological field. Hold tight!"

Luke Soywalker adjusts his controls as he concentrates on the approaching Death Starfish. The spacefish begins to be buffeted and battered slightly.

Breaded Leader instructs, "Switch your shell deflectors on! Double front!"

The tall, dark man finally appeared impatient and walked around some customers sitting at the sushi bar, only to insert himself between other customers once again directly in front of Hiroshi-san. Hiroshi-san looked up from the breaded tibiuo, shook his head, and came face to face with the tall, dark man. Hiroshi-san placed the fin-shaped plate with the accidentally breaded tibiuo sashimi onto the sushi bar next to the tall, dark man's outstretched arms that propped his body up and away from the sushi bar. Hiroshi-san nodded. The tall, dark man just looked at Hiroshi-san with a smirk and would not let his eyes wander. Hiroshi-san, without looking up, began to work on another sushi dish. The air was thick with awkwardness and intimidation.

The spacefish X-Fin fighters, now looking like X-shaped dartfish, move in formation. The Death Starfish now appears to be small, growing rapidly in size as the Rebel fighters approach. Complex patterns on the echinodermic surface begin to become visible. A large dish antenna is built into the surface on one side.

Wedge the Lemontilles is amazed and slightly frightened sour at the awesome spectacle and exclaims, "Look at the size of that thing!"

Breaded Leader interjects, "Cut the batter chatter, Breaded Two! Accelerate to attack speed. This is it, soys!"

The tall, dark man rolled up the sleeves on his black dress shirt, revealing the tattoos of a starfish on each forearm, and replaced his hands on the sushi bar. A very expensive looking and shiny watch was revealed on his left wrist, just below the starfish tattoo.

As the fighters move closer to the Death Starfish, the awesome size of the gargantuan Imperial fortress is revealed. Half of the deadly battle station is in shadow. The remaining area sparkles with thousands of small light pulse reflections running in thin lines and occasionally grouped in large clusters, somewhat like a school of anglerfish as seen from a submersible.

Goma Leader, a battered roll covered in sesame seeds that clammands respect, calls out from his spacefish fishhead, " Breaded Leader, this is Goma Leader."

Breaded Leader responds, "I copy, Goma Leader."

Goma Leader continues, "We're starting for the target mouth and esophagus now."

Hiroshi-san finished preparing a small dish with two raw prawns with only their back shells missing. The crayfish seemingly stared at anyone who looked at the plate. Hiroshi-san moved the breaded tibiuo closer to the edge of the bar and placed the dish with the two prawns on the bar behind the first plate in front of the tall, dark man and said, "For you and... your guest. Both. No charge. And... no deal." Hiroshi-san did not smile. He stared into the eyes of the tall, dark man who continued to stoically stand there. Hiroshi-san moved the plate of breaded tibiuo directly in front of the tall, dark man's hand with the shiny watch, nearly placing it in his hands, and flippantly motioned to take the dishes back to his table. The tall, dark man's smirk gave way to a scowl of anger, disappointment and disgust. His muscles on his arm tensed, making the tattoos rise with his emerging veins.

Breaded Leader looks around at his finmen. The Death Starfish is looming from behind. Two CraY-fin fighters bob back and forth in the oceanverse just beyond. Breaded Leader moves his spacefish brain readout target membrane into position.

He calls out, "We're in position. I'm going to cut across the axis and try to draw their laserbean fire."

Two squads of Rebel fighters peel off. The X-Fins dive towards the Death Starfish surface. A thousand pulse lights seemingly glow across the dark grey expanse of the huge battle station.

The tall, dark man's scowl was followed by a couple of uncontrollable grunts. His face started turning red and his arms became further tensed, his veins coursing and pulsing. The customer sitting near the tall, dark man looked up and became further annoyed and clearly a bit angry. He moved his serving tray containing several pieces of seigo sea bass and bowl of edamame closer to the tall, dark man's right hand in a desperate act to reclaim the space at the sushi bar taken by the tall, dark man's presence. The customer shook his head in a disproving manner, wishing the tall, dark man would just return to his table. The customer scooted his stool closer to the bar and let out an audible 'ahem'.

139

On the Death Starfish, alarm sirens scream as Imperial seigo soldiers scramble to large turbo-powered laserbean gun emplacements. Drivers rotate the huge laserbean guns into position as crawfish adjust their starfish brain targeting devices.

The tall, dark man momentarily looked down at the customer beneath him. This was the first time he took his eyes off Hiroshi-san since standing before him at the sushi bar. His face tensed. His eyes bulged. The tall, dark man raised his right hand and immersed it into the indignant customer's bowl of edamame, pulled out a handful of the beans and backhandedly threw the beans at the customer's face in an unforeseen rage. The edamame bounced off the unsuspecting customer's face and forehead and sprayed across the sushi bar landing on the breaded tibiuo and raw crayfish dishes. A few bounced along the bar and headed our way so, without thinking, I quickly covered my dish with my hand to avoid the flying, stray edamame.

Laserbeans streak through the oceanverse. The Rebel X-Fin fighters move in toward the Imperial plate, as the Death Starfish aims its massive laserbean guns at the Rebel forces and fires. Back on Massassea, Princess Maki and Soy-3PO listen to the battle over the conuslink.
Wedge the Lemontilles calls over the war room conuslink, "Heavy fire, boss! Twenty degrees."
Breaded Leader responds over the conuslink, "I see it. Stay low."

Before the afflicted customer could react, the tall, dark man raised his left hand and slammed it onto the bar, catching the edge of the breaded tibiuo dish possibly by accident, possibly on purpose. The abrupt force on the dish edge launched the accidentally breaded fillets of flying fish up over the tall, dark man's shoulder. Some flew across the room. One fillet hit a different customer on the back of the head at a nearby table. A particularly large fillet hit that same customer's wife on the forehead. The fillet stuck to her face as she let out a scream.

The customer hit in the face with the edamame thrown by the tall, dark man grabbed the dish of seigo and threatened to launch it at the tall, dark man but the tall, dark man grabbed all of the seigo sushi off the plate with his bare hand. He took the plate out of the customer's hand, placed it back on the bar and unceremoniously threw the seigo back on the plate in a motion that expressed his displeasure with the customer. The now irate customer grabbed the leftover edamame in his dish and hurled it at the tall, dark man aimlessly and without reservation, not falling victim to the tall, dark man's intimidation attempts. Hiroshi-san and Junichi-san stood motionless in a complete state of shock. An actual food fight with sushi, at the Moto Sushi bar, had officially started.

An X-Fin zooms across the surface of the Death Starfish.

Inside the Death Starfish, crawfish scurry here and there loading last-minute laserbean armaments and unlocking power noodles.

Wedge the Lemontilles fineuvers his fighter toward the menacing Death Starfish. Other X-Fin fighters continue their attack course on the Death Starfish. Luke Soywalker nosedives radically, starting his attack on the monstrous fortress. The Death Starfish surface streaks past the spacefish's eye.

Luke calls out, "This is Breaded Five. I'm going in!"

Luke's X-Fin fighter races toward the Death Starfish. Laserbeans streak from Luke's weapons, creating a huge bean explosion on the skin surface. Terror crosses Luke's face as he realizes he won't be able to pull out in time to avoid the bean explosion.

Baigai calls out, "Luke, pull up!"

Luke's X-Fin spacefish emerges from the bean explosion, with the leading edges of his fins slightly tarnished in green bean goop.

Baigai asks Luke, "Are you alright?"

Luke adjusts his spacefish nerves and breathes a sigh of relief. Beans burst outside his spacefish's eyes.

Luke replies, "I got beaned, but I'm okay."

The customer nearest the tall, dark man had a confused and shocked expression as he grabbed another handful of the edamame and threw it at the tall, dark man's chest. Some of the edamame ricocheted off his chest and bounced off of his tattooed arms. The tall, dark man was surprised by this insolence and pulled back his arms purely as a defensive maneuver. So doing caused the sake bottle nearest him to waver, wobble and fall onto the sushi bar. It bounced and then bounced again until it hit the surface once again and cracked the top portion of the sake bottle on a nearby dish that held the seigo.

Rebel fighters continue to strafe the Death Starfish's surface with laserbeans. The walls of the Death Starfish start to buckle and, in one section, cave in. Troops and equipment are blown in all directions. Saketroopers stagger out of the rubble. Standing in the middle of the chaos, a vision of calm and foreboding, is Squid Vader. One of his Seigo Officers rushes up to him.

Nearly all of the nearby customers lost their sensibilities and armed themselves with whatever sushi was in front of them, fully blaming the tall, dark man for what was about to occur. Customers from tables behind the tall, dark man grabbed food from nearby dishes and stood up. Customers at the sushi bar lifted off of their stools and grabbed edamame, sushi, and even chopsticks. All of them stood at attention, ready to fire at the tall, dark man if he even so much as moved.

The Seigo Officer informs Squid Vader, "We count thirty Rebel spacefish, Squid Vader, but they're so small they're evading our turbo-laserbeans!"
Squid Vader uncurls a massive tentacle and replies, "We'll have to destroy them spacefish to spacefish. Get the schools to their Gai fighters."

As this was all happening, I noticed the tall, dark man's lady friend was no longer at her table but had somehow managed to sneak up behind me. She quickly ran to the back of the sushi bar and into the kitchen. No one else seemed to really notice this as all attention was on the tall, dark man who was just breathing heavily, glancing at all of the customers out of the corners of his eyes. The lady emerged from the kitchen wearing oven mitts, carrying a steaming pot of clams. She crash landed the pot on the shelves behind the bar, rattling some of the sake bottles on the top shelf, stuck her oven-mitted hand into the scalding water and pulled out a clam. She held it above her head in a threatening position, and waited as she looked around the room. The armed and ready customers all looked at her. It was a standoff.

Steam belches from the giant laserbean guns as they wind up their microwaves to create sufficient power. The schools of saketroopers rush about preparing for another blast. Even the saketroopers cap gear is not adequate to protect them from the overwhelming noise of the monstrous weapon. One saketrooper bangs his cap against the wall in an attempt to stop the ringing.

I looked to my father to try and make sense of what was happening. He was completely focused on the tall, dark man and was angry at the disturbance. He began to shake. My mother grabbed his arm as if to hold him down onto his seat. My father shrugged her off, stood up, pointed at the tall, dark man and yelled, "Get him!" The customer next to him threw a handful of edamame at the tall, dark man. Fish began to fly. Chaos.

Outside of the Death Starfish, the Breaded Leader's X-Fin swims through a heavy hail of laserbean fire and swims past Luke Soywalker as he puts his spacefish nose down and starts his attack dive.

Breaded Leader asks Luke to let him know when he plans to go in.

Luke calls out, "I'm on my way now..."

Breaded Leader responds, "Watch yourself! There's a lot of laserbean fire coming from the right side of that deflection tube foot."

Luke replies, "I'm on it!"

I grabbed some edamame from the bowl in front of me, dunked into my soy sauce and launched it at the tall, dark man. My mother was shocked and was trying to stop my father but quickly realized that was a hopeless mission. One of my edamame hit the tall, dark man on the cheek and left a black smudge of soy sauce on his cheek. He grabbed edamame from the top of the sushi bar and started throwing them about. The lady behind the bar started throwing clams into the crowd of angry customers. Everything started spinning out of control and a very expensive sushi food fight erupted. Hiroshi-san and Junichi-san simply stood there, mouths open, in full shock, not even ducking nearby sushi missiles. My father grabbed a slice of tobiuo and launched it in the direction of the tall, dark man.

Luke flings his X-Fin into a twisting dive across the horizon and down onto the dim grey surface of the Death Starfish. A laserbean shot hurls from Luke's guns. Laserbeans streak toward the onrushing Death Starfish surface. Several small sonar emplacements erupt in sauce. Laserbean fire erupts from a protruding tube foot on the surface of the Death Starfish.

Seeing my dad in action made me smile. I didn't ever think I would see him in a food fight. This was awesome! I know he felt he was defending Hiroshi-san which clearly justified his actions in his own mind.

The blurry Death Starfish surface races past the X-Fin's spacefish eyes as a big smile sweeps across Luke's face at the success of his swim. Laserbean flak plops on all sides of him. The Death Starfish superstructure races past Luke as he fineuvers his craft through a wall of laserbean fire and peels away from the surface towards the vast oceanverse.

The tall, dark man was getting more and more angry. Rage emerged on his face. You could tell he was about to really lose it. I was getting a little frightened.

Inside the Death Starfish, the plop and steam of the big laserbean guns reverberate throughout the massive structure. Many saketroopers rush about in the steam and chaos, silhouetted by the almost continual flash of explosions.

My mother, realizing stopping this was a lost cause, grabbed a handful of baigai from the bowl in front of her and hurled it at the tall, dark man. I continued to throw edamame. Customers from all over the sushi restaurant were throwing whatever they had in front of them at the tall, dark man and some at the lady behind the bar. Hiroshi-san and Junichi-san stood amidst it all, motionless, as if in a trance, not sure what to do.

Meanwhile in his X-Fin fighter, Baigai dives through a reef of sonar domes, antennae, and laserbean gun foot tubes as he shoots low across the Death Starfish surface. A dense barrage of laserbean fire streaks by on all sides. Within the Death Starfish, Imperial spacefish pilots dash in unison to a line of small auxiliary hatches that lead to Imperial Gai fighters.

The lady behind the bar continued to pull out clams from the pot with her oven-mitted hands and threw them at various customers who seemed to be the most threatening to the tall, dark man.

Back on Massassea, Princess Maki, surrounded by her generals and aides, rolls nervously back and forth before a lighted nerve membrane. On all sides technicians work in front of many lighted glass eyes. Udondonna watches quietly from one corner.

One of the officers working over a nerve membrane speaks into his antenna headset, "Squad leaders, we've picked up a new group of signals. Enemy fighters coming your way."

Luke Soywalker looks around to see if he can spot the approaching

Imperial gai fighters but doesn't and reports, "My eye-scope's negative. I don't see anything."

Out of the corner of his eye, my father caught a flying clam whizzing by. He began to look for who was throwing the clams as he realized the lady behind the bar was aiming at the customers. Edamame thrown by customers on the other side of the tall, dark man missed and hit my father, causing him to raise his arms in defense and duck.

The Death Starfish's surface sweeps past as Breaded Leader searches for Imperial fighters. Laserbean flak pounds at his spacefish.
Breaded Leader clammands, "Keep up your visual scanning. With all this jamming, they'll be on top of you before your eye-scope can pick them up."

I looked over at the lady behind the sushi bar and saw her watch my mom throw baigai at the tall, dark man. She scowled and grabbed a handful of clams from the pot and launched them in our direction. My father saw this and called out, "Watch it!"
My mother looked confused amidst a hailstorm of flying edamame and clams. She then finally looked at the lady behind the bar with her mouth wide open. She didn't know what to do. My mom then formed a scowl on her face. I've seen that look before. The lady was now in trouble.

Suddenly four ferocious gai fighter ships dive on the Rebel fighters. Two of the gai fighters peel off and drop out. The other two hurl towards Baigai.
Baigai panics when he discovers a gai fighter on his shell. The horizon in the background twists around as he peels off, hoping to lose the gai fighter.
Breaded Leader calls out to Baigai, "Baigai! You've picked one up… watch it!"
Baigai responds in a panic, "I can't see it! Where is he?!"
Baigai zooms off the surface and into the oceanverse, closely followed by an Imperial gai fighter. The gai fighter fires several laserbeans at Baigai, but misses. Baigai sees the gai fighter behind him and swings around, trying to avoid him.
He calls out, "He's on me tight! I can't shake him! I can't shake him!"
Baigai, swimming at high seas, peels off and dives toward the Death Starfish surface, but he is unable to lose the gai fighter sticking close to

his shell. Luke Soywalker is swimming upside down. He rotates his spacefish around to normal seas as he comes out of his dive.

He calls out to Baigai, " Hang on, Baigai! I'm coming in."

One of the clams the lady threw was heading straight for my mother's head so I threw my hands up to block it. The clam ricocheted off my hands and splattered onto the bar into a watery, slimy mess. I yelled out, "Got it!"

Now I was mad too.

Baigai and the tailing gai fighter dive for the surface, now followed by a fast-gaining Luke. After Baigai dives out of sight, Luke chases the Imperial fighter. The gai fighter races across the surface of the Death Starfish now closely followed by Luke's X-Fln fighter. Luke shoots at the gai fighter and hits it. It explodes into slimy pieces.

Luke yells out, "Got him!"

The tall, dark man, avoiding items thrown at him, then made his way around the other side of the bar, passed Hiroshi-san and Junichi-san who were both now yelling at the customers and waving their hands to try and stop the food fight. The tall, dark man stood next to the lady by the shelf of sake, submerged his bare hands into the once boiling water in the pot and grabbed some clams. I grabbed some of my mom's tobiuo and threw it at the tall, dark man. As I did, I got hit in the face by some stray edamame. I jerked back in reaction and spilled my miso soup all over my other hand which was laying flat on the bar surface. The tall, dark man and his lady friend launched more clams across the restaurant.

Squid Vader strides purposefully down the Death Starfish's ring canal, flanked by the Imperial saketroopers. Vader clammands, " Several fighters have broken off from the main groupers. Come with me!"

A concerned Princess Maki, Soy-3PO, Udondonna, and other officers of the Rebellion stand around the huge round nerve membrane, listening to the spacefish-to-spacefish communication on the room's loudspeaker. They hear Baigai call out, "Pull in! Luke, pull in!" and then Wedge the Lemontilles say, "Watch your back! Gai fighter's above you, coming in!"

Luke's X-Fln soars away from the Death Starfish's surface as he spots the tailing gai fighter. The gai fighter takes aim at Luke's X-Fin and scores a laserbean hit on Luke's X-Fln. Steam emerges from the right side of the X-Fin. Luke looks out from the spacefish eyes at the steam and calls in, "I'm hit, but not bad. Now, I'm steamed!" Steam pours out from beyond Miso-D2.

Luke instructs, "Miso-D2, see what you can do with it. Hang on back there."

Green laserbean fire moves past the gurgling roebot as his top bowl turns. Luke nervously works his spacefish's nerve endings. Back on Massassea, Princess Maki stands frozen as she listens and worries about Luke.

Breaded Leader calls out over the antenna, "Breaded Six... Can you see Breaded Five?"

Breaded Ten responds, "There's a heavy laserbean fire zone on this side. Breaded Five, where are you?"

Luke spots the gai fighter behind him and swims away from the Death Starfish surface.

He calls out, "I can't shake him!"

Luke's spacefish swims closer to the surface of the Death Starfish with an Imperial gai fighter closing in on him in hot pursuit. The Death Starfish whips below Wedge the Lemontilles as he swims into view. He calls out, "I'm on him, Luke! Hold on!" Wedge the Lemontilles dives across the horizon toward Luke and the gai fighter, moving his X-Fin in rapidly. Luke reacts frantically and responds, "Blast it! Wedge, where are you?"

The saketrooper in the tailing gai fighter watches Wedge the Lemontilles approach in his X-Fin as another X-Fin joins him. Both unleash a volley of laserbean fire on the Imperial fighter. The gai fighter separates, filling the area with a slimy, clammy goo. Luke's spacefish swims off into the distance.

A relieved Luke calls in his thanks to the team.

Baigai calls in, "Good shooting, Wedge!"

More sushi and other random food items soar through the air toward the tall, dark man and his lady companion from all angles of the sushi restaurant.

Goma Leader peels off and starts toward the long grooves at the Death Starfish surface and chimes in, "Breaded Leader, this is Goma Leader. We're starting our attack run." Three CraY-Fin fighters of the Goma group dive out of the oceanverse toward the Death Starfish surface. Princess Maki and the others are grouped around the nerve center table at Massassea as technicians move about attending to their duties.

Breaded Leader responds, "I copy, Goma Leader. Move into position."

147

The tall, dark man picks up three clams and arranges them on his arm, cradling them. The customer sitting next to my dad leaned over the sushi bar and grabbed a handful of sesame seeds from an open container near where Hiroshi-san was jumping up and down. The customer then yelled something at the tall, dark man in Japanese and launched the seeds toward the tall, dark man's face. Hiroshi-san, seeing this unfolding, was close enough to interfere and tried to block the customer's throw. At the same time, the lady threw edamame at the customer. Hiroshi-san hit the customer's hand as it was in motion which then caused the seeds to scatter aimlessly about the floor behind the sushi bar. This incident made the tall, dark man crack an evil smile and laugh as if he had already won.

Three Imperial gai fighters, in precise clammation, dive toward the Death Starfish surface. Squid Vader, inside his Advanced Gai-1 Fighter spacefish, calmly adjusts his control nerve as the plates whip past the clam opening.

Squid Vader clammands, "Stay in attack clammation!"

Goma Leader lines up with something on the Death Starfish's surface and calls out, "The mouth and esophagus are... marked and locked in!" Goma Leader approaches the Death Starfish and pulls out to skim the surface. The spacefish moves into a deep ambulacral groove, firing laserbeans. The surface streaks past as laserbean fire is returned by the Death Starfish. Goma Five, an older and battered roll covered in sesame seeds in the formation, looks around to see if enemy spacefish are near. His CraY-Fin fighter is buffeted by Imperial laserbean flak.

Goma Leader swooshes down the enormous ambulacral groove that leads to the mouth and esophagus. Laserbeans blast toward him in increasing numbers, occasionally exploding near the spacefish causing it to bounce about. He clammands the spacefish to switch power to the front deflector gills. The three CraY-Fins continue to skim the Death Starfish surface as laserbeans streak past on all sides. An exterior surface laserbean gun blazes away at the oncoming Rebel fighters.

Goma Leader calls out, "How many laserbean guns do you think, Goma Five?"

Goma Five responds, "I'd say about twenty laserbeans. Most on the surface."

On Massassea, Princess Maki, Soy-3PO, and the technicians view the projected target nerve endings, as red and blue target pulses glow. The red target pulse near the center blinks on and off. On the overhead conuslink, an announcement is heard saying, "Death Starfish will be in range in five seconds."

The three CraY-Fins swoosh through a hail of laserbean fire. Goma

Two, a younger roll covered in sesame seeds, pulls down his targeting antenna and adjusts it. His spacefish shudders under intense laserbean barrage.

Goma Two informs, "I'm locked. Getting a pulse."

As the fighters begin to approach the target mouth and esophagus area, suddenly all the laserbean fire stops. An eerie calm hovers over the ambulacral groove as the surface continues to whip across in a blur.

Goma Two continues, "The laserbean guns, they've stopped!"

Goma Five looks behind him.

Goma Leader yells, "They're coming in! Three marks at two ten!"

Three Imperial gai fighter spacefish with Squid Vader in the center flanked by two finmen, dive in precise clammation almost vertically toward the Death Starfish surface. Squid Vader calmly adjusts his control nerve with his tentacles as the plates zoom by.

Squid Vader proclaims, "I'll take them myself! Cover me!"

One of the saketroopers respond, "Yes, sir!"

Three gai fighters zoom across the surface of the Death Starfish. Squid Vader lines up Goma Two in his targeting nerve. His tentacles grip the control nerve as he presses the clampedo button. The CraY-Fin spacefish brain explodes around Goma Two. His seeds fall forward off his roll and scatter to the floor. As Goma Two's spacefish explodes, shell and seed debris is flung into the oceanverse. Goma Leader looks over his own roll of seeds at the scene. The three gai fighters race along in the ambulacral groove in a tight clammation.

Goma Leader panics as cries out, "I can't fineuver!"

Goma Five tries to calm Goma Leader down by saying, "Stay on target!"

The Death Starfish races by, outside the spacefish brain, as he adjusts his targeting nerve and says, "We're too close!" The older pile of seeds remains calm and repeats, "Stay on target!" Goma Leader really starts panicking as he exclaims, "Loosen up!"

Squid Vader calmly adjusts his targeting nerve and pushes the clampedo button once more. Goma Leader's CraY-Fin spacefish is hit by Squid Vader's laserbean. Goma Leader explodes in a ball of shell and seed, throwing debris in all directions.

Goma Five moves in on the exhaust mouth and calls in, "Goma Five to Breaded Leader..."

Luke Soywalker looks over his shoulder at the action outside of his X-Fin spacefish brain.

Goma Five continues, "Lost Tori. Lost Dashi."

Breaded Leader solemnly replies, "I copy, Goma Five."

Goma Five continues, "They came from behind..."

One of the crayfish legs explodes on Goma Five's CraY-Fin fighter, throwing shell bits everywhere. He dives past the horizon toward the Death Starfish's surface, passing a gai fighter during his descent. Goma

Five, a veteran roll of countless campaigns, spins toward the fryer.

The tall, dark man continued to laugh to himself.

12 VICTORY AT SEA

The Moto Sushi restaurant was in complete chaos. There were maybe twenty customers around the restaurant grabbing various food items and throwing them at the tall, dark man and his lady friend. One woman in the back corner was on her cell phone, covering one ear and shouting. Another young couple was laughing in disbelief and filming the entire scene on their smartphones. Then there was one older man in the center of it all, sitting calmly, eating tarako spaghetti and seemed to not even be aware that there was a full-out food fight going on around him. He didn't look up. He didn't notice anything. He just ate his food. Acting completely normal amidst the chaos appeared entirely strange to me. With all of this going on, I started getting a little concerned, especially since my parents got involved. I've never seen them like this. This was getting serious. The tall, dark man continued to laugh with an evil grin.

Luke Soywalker looks nervously around him at the explosive battle between the Goma Squadron and the gai fighters.

Grand Moff Tarako and a Chief Seigo Officer stand in the Death Starfish brain cavity.

The Chief Seigo Officer informs, "We've analyzed their attack, sir, and there is a danger. Should I have your spacefish standing by?"

Grand Moff Tarako replies, "Evacuate? In our moment of triumph? I think you overestimate their chances!"

Grand Moff Tarako turns to the Death Starfish brain nerve readout, pleased with what he sees. The conuslink echoes, "Rebel secret plate, three minutes and closing."

Breaded Leader looks over at his finmen, and calls, "Breaded Group, this is Breaded Leader."

Udondonna moves to the conuslink at Massassea as he fiddles with the nerve endings.

Breaded Leader clammands, "Rendezvous at mark six point one."

Wedge the Lemontilles replies, "This is Breaded Two. Swimming toward you."

Baigai replies next, "Breaded Three, standing by..."

Udondonna chimes in, "Breaded Leader, this is Plate One. Keep half of your group out of range for the next swim."

Breaded Leader confirms, "Copy, Plate One. Luke, take Breaded Two and Three. Hold up here and wait for my signal... to start your swim."

Luke confirms.

As the food fight was going on around me, I kept low as to not get pegged by flying sushi and to make sure the tall, dark man and his lady friend did not notice me. I snuck behind my mother and collected the tobiuo sashimi. I took three pieces and placed them on a small serving plate. Then, staying low, I made my way to the edge of the bamboo wall and situated myself halfway into the hallway to the bathrooms. I looked around the corner of the hallway toward the kitchen area and saw the tall, dark man and lady discuss something very quickly as they dodged various food items. They then started lobbing more clams at customers. At this point, Hiroshi-san transitioned from shock to pure anger. He was visibly shaking as he watches disaster strike his business.

The X-Fin fighters of Luke, Baigai, and Wedge the Lemontilles swim in formation high above the Death Starfish's surface. Luke peers out from the spacefish's eyes. Two X-Fins move across the surface of the Death Starfish. Breaded Leader's X-Fin drops down to the surface leading to the mouth and esophagus. Breaded Leader looks around to watch for the gai fighters. He begins to drop seeds from his roll.

Breaded Leader calls out, "This is it!"

Hiroshi-san waved his hands in the air and began to approach the tall, dark man and finally got his attention. He became very focused on what Hiroshi-san was going to do. I took advantage of the situation and flung tobiuo sashimi pieces at the tall, dark man. The lady beside the man saw this and grabbed another handful of edamame and threw them in my direction.

Breaded Leader roams down the ambulacral groove of the Death Starfish as laserbeans streak across the oceanverse. A huge laserbean cannon fires at the approaching Rebel X-Fin fighters. The Rebel fighters evade the Imperial laserbean blasts. Breaded Ten looks around for the Imperial fighters.

Breaded Ten says, "We should be able to see it by now."

From the spacefish fishheads, the surface of the Death Starfish streaks by, with Imperial laserbean fire shooting toward them.

Breaded Leader advises, "Keep your eyes open for those fighters!"

Breaded Ten calls out, "There's too much interference!"

The three X-Fin fighters move in formation down the Death Starfish ambulacral groove.

Breaded Ten asks, "Breaded Five, can you see them from where you are?"

Luke looks down at the Death Starfish surface and informs, "No sign of any... wait! Coming in point three five."

The tall, dark man turned toward me, took the three clams off of his cradling arm and hurled them in my direction.

Breaded Ten looks up and sees the Imperial fighters and informs the squadron. Three gai fighters, Squid Vader flanked by two finmen, dive in a tight clammation. Breaded Leader pulls his targeting antenna in front of his seed eyes and makes several adjustments.

Breaded Leader calls out, "I'm in range. Target's coming up."

Breaded Leader's X-Fin moves up the Death Starfish ambulacral groove. He looks at his target nerve readout and then looks in the targeting nerve.

"Just hold them off for a few seconds," clammands Breaded Leader.

Squid Vader adjusts his clam control lever and dives on the X-Fin fighters and instructs, "Close up clammation."

The three gai fighters move in clammation across the Death Starfish surface. Breaded Leader lines up the target mouth on the targeting nerve. Squid Vader and his finmen zoom down the ambulacral groove.

Squid Vader rapidly approaches the two X-Fins of Breaded Ten and Breaded Twelve. Squid Vader's laserbean cannon flashes beans from within the two clam shells. The X-Fins show up in the targeting nerve of the clam spacefish. Breaded Ten works at his nerve endings furiously, trying to avoid Squid Vader's clam fighter behind him.

Breaded Ten panics and says, "You'd better let her loose!" Breaded Leader is concentrating on his targeting nerve and informs, "Almost there!"

Breaded Ten yells out, "I can't hold them!"

One of the tobiuo sashimi pieces that I threw at the tall, dark man hit the sushi bar shelf and splat there. It clung to the glass under the shelf for a second and then oozed onto the bar surface. My second sashimi missile went high and hit the sake bottles on the shelf behind the tall, dark man, rattled the bottles and then unceremoniously fell to the floor next to a limp piece of kushikatsu that some other customer must have thrown.

Squid Vader and his finmen continue their pursuit as they whip through the ambulacral groove after the X-Fins. Squid Vader calmly pushes the clampedo button on his control nerve. His well-aimed laserbean fire proves to be unavoidable and strikes Breaded Ten's spacefish. Breaded Ten screams in anguish and pain as his X-Fin splits apart and bursts into fish flesh bits. Grimly, Breaded Leader takes careful aim and watches his targeting nerve which shows the target mouth lined up in the crosshairs. He fires his laserbeans.

Breaded Leader calls out, "It's away!"

Inside the Death Starfish, an Imperial saketrooper is knocked to the floor from the attack's bean explosion. Other saketroopers scurrying about the ring canal are knocked against the canal wall and lose their balance.

Princess Maki and the others stare at the nerve endings before them back on Massassea hoping to learn of success from the attack.

Breaded Nine excitedly yells, "It's a hit!"

Breaded Leader replies, "Negative."

Breaded Leader looks back at the receding Death Starfish. Tiny bean explosions are visible in the distance.

Breaded Leader continues, "Negative! It didn't go in. It just impacted on the surface."

Squid Vader peels off in pursuit as Breaded Leader's X-Fin passes the Death Starfish horizon. Squid Vader swings his spacefish around for the next fry.

Luke advises, "Breaded Leader, we're right above you. Turn to point..."

He tries to spot Breaded Leader and looks down at the Death Starfish surface.

Luke continues, "...oh five. We'll cover for you."

Breaded Leader looks about nervously and clammands, "Stay there... I just lost my starboard gill."

Luke looks anxiously toward Breaded Leader's X-Fin.

Breaded Leader says, "Get set to make your attack swim."

Squid Vader's gloved tentacles make contact with the clam control nerves. He presses their laserbean firing buttons. Breaded Leader fights to gain control of his spacefish. Laserbeans emit from Squid Vader's advanced gai fighter and connect with Breaded Leader's X-Fin. Breaded Leader is hit, screams, and splats into a beaned ball of fish guts and pork rinds.

Luke looks out the eyes of his X-Fin spacefish at the bean explosion far below. For the first time, he feels the helplessness of his situation.

The tall, dark man easily avoided the sashimi lobbed in his direction. I should have planned my attack a bit better. Other customers continued to hurl fish at him and not much was hitting him. In fact, I only saw a few pieces hit him and they insignificantly bounced off. He shrugged them off completely. Hiroshi-san tried to talk with the tall, dark man and convince him to stop all of this madness. He ignored him at first. Then he grabbed Hiroshi-san by the arm and threw him into the kitchen. He was physically no match for the tall, dark man. His lady friend was laughing sinisterly at Hiroshi-san.

The tall, dark man then told his lady friend to go into the kitchen after Hiroshi-san and tell him this shame will continue until he decides to close the restaurant. She nodded and went into the kitchen.

Grand Moff Tarako casts a sinister roe at the nerve endings before him on the Death Starfish.

The conuslink overhead echoes, "Rebel secret plate, one minute and closing."

At Massassea, Udondonna and Princess Maki, with Soy-3PO beside them, listen intently to the talk between the X-Fin fighters. The room is grim after Breaded Leader's demise. Princess Maki nervously rolls about the room.

Luke calls out to the remaining squadron, "Baigai, Wedge the Lemontilles, let's close it up. We're going in. We're going in full fin throttle."

Wedge the Lemontilles pulls out and replies, "Right with you, boss."

The two X-Fins peel off against the oceanverse and dive toward the Death Starfish.

Baigai asks, "Luke at that speed will you be able to pull out in time?"

Luke replies, "It'll be just like Bamboo's Canyon back home."

The three remaining X-Fins move in, unleashing a barrage of laserbean fire. Laserbean fire is returned from the Death Starfish. Luke's lifelong friend struggles with his X-Fin nerve controls.

Baigai calls out, "We'll stay back far enough to cover you."

Laserbean flak flash about outside of Luke's spacefish.

Wedge the Lemontilles advises, "My eye-scope shows the tube foot, but I can't see the mouth opening! Are you sure the spacefish brain nerves can hit it?"

The Death Starfish laserbean cannon slowly rotates as it shoots laserbeans. Luke looks around for the Imperial gai fighters. He thinks for a moment and then moves his targeting nerve into position.

Luke warns, "Watch yourself! Increase speed to full fin throttle!"

Wedge the Lemontilles looks excitedly about for any sign of the gai fighters.

Wedge asks, "What about the tube foot?"

Luke corrects, "You worry about those fighters! I'll worry about the tube foot!"

Luke's X-Fin streaks through the ambulacral groove firing laserbeans at the surface. Luke breaks into a nervous soy sweat as the laserbean fire is returned, nicking one of his fins close to the gills.

Luke shouts, "Miso-D2! That, that stabilizer fin has broken loose again! See if you can't lock it down!"

Miso-D2 works to repair the damages to the X-Fin. The ambulacral groove wall rushes by as he executes the delicate task. Two laserbean cannons are firing on the Rebel fighters. Wedge the Lemontilles looks up and sees the gai fighters. Luke's targeting nerve marks off the distance to the target. Squid Vader and his finmen zoom closer. Squid Vader adjusts his nerve controls and fires laserbeans at two X-Fins swimming down the ambulacral groove. He scores a direct hit on Wedge the Lemontilles.

Princess Maki and the others are still grouped around the nerve endings at Massassea.

Wedge the Lemontilles calls out, "I'm hit! I can't stay with you."
Luke replies, "Get clear, Wedge! You can't do any more good back there!"

Wedge the Lemontilles responds, "Sorry!"

He pulls his crippled X-Fin spacefish back away from the battle. Squid Vader watches the escape but issues a clammand to his finmen.

Squid Vader clammands, "Let him go! Stay on the leader!"

I left my post at the corner of the bathroom hallway and ran to the bar by my mother who was now ducking under the bar. I grabbed a handful of her baigai water snails and launched them at the tall, dark man before running back to the corner of the hallway. The water snails hit the tall, dark man in the chest and arms and splattered to the floor. The tall, dark man looked at me and then crushed the snails with his foot as he snarled at me.

Luke's X-Fin speeds down the ambulacral groove. The three gai fighters, still in perfect unbroken clammation, tail close behind. Baigai looks around at the gai fighters. He is worried.

Baigai warns, "Hurry, Luke. They're coming in much faster this time. I can't hold them!"

The three gai fighters move ever closer to Luke and Baigai. Luke looks back anxiously at Miso-D2.

He calls out, "Miso-D2, try and increase gill power!"

Ignoring the bumpy ride, laserbean flak, a gurgling Miso-D2 struggles to increase the gill power, his top bowl turning from side to side. Stealthily, the gai clammation creeps closer. Squid Vader adjusts his nerve controls. Baigai looks around at the gai fighters. Luke looks into his targeting nerve and moves it away for a moment and ponders its use. He looks back into the targeting nerve.

Baigai warns again, "Hurry up, Luke!"

Squid Vader and his finmen race through the Death Starfish ambulacral groove. Baigai moves in to cover for Luke, but Squid Vader gains on him. Baigai sees the gai fighter aiming at him.

Baigai screams out, "Wait!"

Squid Vader squeezes the laserbean fire button on his nerve controls. Baigai's spacefish brain explodes around him. Baigai's spacefish bursts into a million bits of fish and snail. Shell and fish guts fall to the surface.

Princess Maki and the others stare at the nerve endings before them in disbelief. Luke is stunned by Baigai's frying. His roe eyes are watering but his anger is also growing.

The lady emerged from the kitchen with Hiroshi-san and was using him as a human shield against all the foods flying in their direction. She was whispering in his ear the entire time. Hiroshi-san resigned by nodding and started to raise his hands and yelled out to his customers, "Stop! Please stop! This is not going to solve anything! Please stop!" However, the customers were so worked up, most of them hadn't even heard or noticed him. Others were simply ducking below the sushi bar to avoid clams being flung out by the tall, dark man and didn't even realize Hiroshi-san was in the line of fire. He was getting pelted by random pieces of food. This made me angry. Hiroshi-san didn't deserve this.

Grand Moff Tarako watches the projected nerve endings on the Death Starfish with satisfaction. The overhead conuslink calls out, "Rebel secret plate, thirty seconds and closing."

Squid Vader takes aim on Luke and talks to the finmen. He informs, "I'm on the leader."

Luke's X-Fin spacefish streaks through the ambulacral groove of the Death Starfish. Princess Maki returns her general's worried and doubtful glances with solid, grim determination. Soy-3PO seems more nervous than usual and utters, "Hang on, Miso-D2!"

At the height of the chaos, Junichi-san crawled along the floor behind the front of the sushi bar, carrying what appeared to be drinking straws between his teeth. He headed my way avoiding customers and falling pieces of fish and shells. He was also carrying something in his left hand as he crawled over to my stool. He sat on the floor with his back propped up against the back of the sushi bar between my stool and my ducking mother. My mother said something to him, but he clearly couldn't hear her or simply didn't understand what she was saying. He then looked around and caught my eye. He smiled and in so doing dropped the drinking straws he was holding between his teeth into his right hand. He held up a small burlap bag with his left hand and the straws in his right and motioned both of them to me by moving his hands in my direction. I looked at him in a confused manner and then realized he wanted to give me these items. I looked above the bar from around the corner and made sure the coast was clear.

I hurriedly crawled on all fours to where Junichi-san was sitting. He handed me the straws and the bag. he then said, "Billy-san, use rice! Use rice!" He pointed above his head motioning at the tall, dark man and his lady accomplice behind the bar. He then motioned the straw to his mouth and made his cheeks puff out. I nodded. My mother called out, "Billy, no! Stay low!" I ignored her, took the burlap bag of rice and the straws and made my way back to the hallway corner.

Luke concentrates on his targeting nerve. Three gai fighters charge away down the ambulacral groove toward Luke. Squid Vader's tentacles curl around the control nerve. Luke adjusts the nerve ending of his targeting nerve. Luke's ships charges down the ambulacral groove. He lines up the nerve ending's crosshairs. He looks into the targeting nerve and then hears a familiar voice.

Zen Wasabi's voice calls out, "Use the Rice, Luke."

The Death Starfish ambulacral groove zooms by. Luke looks up and then starts to look back into the targeting nerve. He has second thoughts.

Zen's voice calls out again, "Let go, Luke."

A grim determination sweeps across Luke's soy face as he closes his eyes and starts to mumble Zen's training to himself. Luke's X-FIn fighter streaks through the ambulacral groove.

Squid Vader comments to himself, "The Rice is strong with this one!"

Squid Vader follows Luke's X-Fin down the ambulacral groove. Luke

looks to the targeting nerve, then away as he hears Zen's voice.
Zen Wasabi's voice calls out again, "Luke, trust me."
Luke moves the targeting nerve away and back into its brain hold.

My mother called out to me again, "Billy! Billy! Get over here right now! I don't want you getting clammed!" I just yelled back at her, "I'm alright, mom! I'm fine!"

A Rebel clammander at the Massassea secret plate calls in to Luke, "His spacefish's brain is off. Luke, you switched off your targeting nerve. What's wrong?"
Luke replies, "Nothing. I'm alright."

My father was still lobbing food at the tall, dark man but had retreated back to the tables in the corner of the restaurant where the woman on her cell phone was. He was picking up any available food items and simply randomly hurling it in the general direction of the bar.

The tall, dark man then grabbed a handful of edamame from behind the bar and launched it out in my direction but the bold Hiroshi-san grabbed his arm while it was in motion. The edamame was let go prematurely and ended up hitting the ceiling and spraying down along the sushi bar. Several of the beans splash landed in my miso soup and spilled it onto the bar.

Luke's spacefish streaks ever closer to the target mouth. Luke looks at the Death Starfish surface streaking by. Miso-D2 turns his top bowl from side to side, burping in anticipation. The three gai fighters, finned by Squid Vader and his two finmen, follow Luke's X-Fin down the ambulacral groove. Squid Vader fineuvers his nerve controls as he looks at his doomed target. He presses the fire buttons on his nerve controls. Laserbean fire streams toward Luke's X-Fin fighter. A large burst of Squid Vader's laserbean fire engulfs Miso-D2. His top bowl tilts to the side and falls limp as he emits a high-pitched sound as steam escapes his bowl. Luke looks frantically back at Miso-D2. Steam billows out around Miso-D2 and soy begins to fly about. Miso-D2's burping and gurgling sounds die out.
Luke calls out, "I've lost Miso-D2!"
Princess Maki and the others stare intently at the nerve endings while Soy-3PO watches the princess. Lights representing the Death Starfish and targets glow brightly on the nerve endings.

The tall, dark man then shoved Hiroshi-san away from him. Hiroshi-san slipped as he was forced back and hit his head on the sushi bar. He collapsed behind the bar. The tall, dark man then came out from behind the bar by my stool and looked down at my mother. He got hit in the head with a random piece of raw fish which confused him a bit. He looked around and saw me looking at him from behind the hallway corner.

A voice overhead on the conuslink announces, "The Death Starfish has cleared the plates. The Death Starfish has cleared the plates."

Grand Moff Tarako glares at the nerve endings as the overhead conuslink announces, "Rebel secret plate, in range."

Grand Moff Tarako clammands, "You may fire when ready."

The conuslink responds, "Commence primary ignition."

A Seigo Officer reaches up and pushes buttons on the nerve controls within the Death Starfish.

The three gai fighters zoom down the Death Starfish ambulacral groove in pursuit of Luke, never breaking clammation. Luke looks anxiously at the target mouth. Squid Vader adjusts his nerve controls, checking his projected targeting nerve. Luke's spacefish barrels down the ambulacral groove. Squid Vader's targeting nerve swings around in position. He takes careful aim on Luke's X-Fin. He pushes the laserbean fire buttons on the nerve controls. The three gai fighters move in on Luke. As Squid Vader's center fighter unleashes a volley of laserbean, one of the gai fighters at his side is hit and explodes into gooey shell fragments. The two remaining gai fighters continue to move in. Luke looks about, wondering whose laserbean fire destroyed Squid Vader's finman. Squid Vader is taken by surprise and looks out from the clamshells as he mutters, "What?" Squid Vader's finman searches around him trying to locate the unknown attacker.

As the customers in the sushi bar started running out of things to throw, the door to the restaurant opened and a police officer entered. The woman in the back corner who had been on her cell phone the whole time, motioned to him as he entered. She ran up to him and was frantically explaining what was going on. The police officer looked very confused and was ducking random pieces of flying fish bits. The tall, dark man hadn't noticed that a police officer had entered.

I realized that my mom was in danger now. Once the tall, dark man saw the police officer, he might take a hostage to escape and my mom was the closest person to him, shuddering and shaking under the sushi bar. My father must have seen that Hiroshi-san fell behind the bar, because he grabbed a bowl of edamame off of a nearby table and flung the entire bowl across the restaurant toward the lady behind the bar. As it flew across the room, edamame sprayed out randomly from the bowl pelting customers, tables, and other items on the tables along the way. The bowl flew like a frisbee and hit the top of the sushi bar, ricocheted up and smacked the lady right in the forehead. She was stunned, looked cross-eyed, and fell onto the shelves of sake, rattling them back and forth as she slumped to the ground, bottles of sake falling in her direction, bonking her on the head. She was out.

From within the Millennium Flounder, Prawn Solo and Unagibacca grin excitedly.

Prawn Solo yells, "Yahoo!"

The Millennium Flounder heads right at the two gai fighters on a collision course. The finman spots the pirate spacefish coming at him and warns the Dark Lord of the Surf by yelling, "Look out!"

Squid Vader's finman panics at the sight of the oncoming pirate spacefish and veers radically to one side, colliding with Squid Vader's gai fighter in the process. Squid Vader's finman crashes into the side wall of the ambulacral groove and explodes into buts of shell, glass, and clammy goop. Squid Vader's damaged spacefish spins out of the ambulacral groove with a badly damaged shell and heads for the deep oceanverse. He turns round and round in circles with a cracked and sheared shell, heading deeper and deeper into the oceanverse.

Prawn Solo's spacefish moves in toward the Death Starfish ambulacral groove. Prawn, smiling, speaks to Luke over his antenna, "You're all clear, soy."

Princess Maki and the others listen to Prawn Solo's tidemission.

Prawn Solo calls out to Luke, "Now let's blow this thing and go home!"

The tall, dark man looked behind him and realized the lady was knocked out cold, slumped behind the bar, lying next to Hiroshi-san. He turned and looked around. He looked furious. At that point, he realized there was a policeman in the restaurant. The policeman was still talking to the woman from the back corner as she was pointing excitedly at the tall, dark man. The tall, dark man looked around and glanced down at my mother. Uh oh.

I took a handful of rice out of the burlap bag, jammed the rice into the straw Junichi-san gave me and put the straw to my mouth. The rice fell out. I looked on the table nearest to me and saw a bowl of ponzu sauce. I loaded the straw with the rice once again, plugged the end with my finger, and poured some of the ponzu sauce into the straw to expand the rice. I placed the straw to my mouth once again but it was bitter. I tried to focus and concentrate on my target, but then pulled the straw out from my mouth thinking the policeman would be better suited to handle this. Junichi-san yelled out, "Billy-san, no! Trust me! Use rice! Now!"

I put the straw back near my mouth, took a very deep breath, aimed for the tall, dark man's head and blew into the straw with all my might. Several soaked rice grains flew threw the air. The tall, dark man looked up, glanced at me, saw the rice approaching him at very high speed, and opened his mouth in disbelief.

The grains of ponzu-soaked rice flying through the air, pelted the tall, dark man's face. Some of the grains clearly must have entered his mouth and disappeared into his esophagus. The tall, dark man started gagging. He grabbed his throat and wheezed. He spun around and coughed. He gasped for air. He wheezed again and coughed violently. He spun around again to the bar and grabbed a glass of water and gargled it. He spit the water up out of his mouth and sprayed it all around, coughing even more. As he spun around again, he slipped on the wet floor, spun again, bonked his head on the sushi bar, and fell to the floor. He moaned, moaned again louder, and then threw up all over the floor and passed out.

The policeman got to him just as he had thrown up and had to jump back to avoid getting vomit on his shiny, black shoes.

Luke looks up and smiles. He concentrates on the exhaust mouth, then fires his ponzu sauce torpedoes. Luke's ponzu sauce torpedoes shoot toward the mouth and seems to simply disappear into the surface and not explode. But the shots do find their mark and have gone into the target mouth and are heading for the pyloric stomach. Luke throws back in relief.

A saketrooper runs to the nerve controls and pulls the attack nerve ending as the brain behind him lights up.

The conuslink in the Death Starfish calls out, "Stand by to fire at Rebel secret plate."

Two X-Fins, a CraY-Fin and the Millennium Flounder race toward Yafin in the distance.

Several saketroopers, flanking a pensive Grand Moff Tarako, busily push control nerves.

The conuslink echoes, "Standing by."

The rumble of a distant explosion begins.

The Rebel spacefish race out of sight leaving the massive Death Starfish alone against the black of the oceanverse. Several small flashes appear on the surface. The Death Starfish bursts into a supertide, creating a spectacular display of launched shrapnel in all directions. It exploded in spectacular fashion.

Junichi-san comforted my mother by holding her arm and helping her up to her feet. All of the customers in the sushi bar had stopped throwing food items. The policeman handcuffed the tall, dark man as he lay on the floor unconscious. He then went behind the bar and handcuffed the lady as well as she was waking up. He helped her to her feet. Hiroshi-san helped himself up from the floor at the same time using the bar as an aid to lift himself. The policeman radioed for other officers to come and assist as he held the lady and placed her in a chair. Junichi-san looked over to me to make sure I was ok and said, "Great shot, Billy-san! You shoot! You shoot it good! Rice always good for you!"

Prawn Solo calls out, "Great shot, soy! That was one in a million."
Luke is at ease and his eyes are closed.
Zen Wasabi's voice breaks his silence, "Remember, the Rice will be with you... always... because it's sticky! "
The spacefish rocks back and forth.
Meanwhile, Squid Vader's damaged advanced gai fighter spins off into the oceanverse.
The Rebel spacefish race toward the fourth dish of Yafin, to Massassea. When they finally land back at the Rebel secret plate, Luke climbs out of his X-Fin and is cheered by a throng of ground crew of groupers. Luke climbs down as they all welcome him with laughter, cheers, and shouting. Princess Maki rushes toward him.
She exclaims, "Luke! Luke! Luke!"
She throws her nori around Luke and hugs him as they dance around in a circle. Prawn Solo runs in toward Luke and they embrace one another, slapping each other on the back with pink-shelled legs and globs of soy.
He shouts and laughs, "Hey! Hey!"
Luke says, "I knew you'd come back! I just knew it!"
Prawn replies, "Well, I wasn't gonna let you get all the credit and take all the cowry shells!"
Luke and Prawn Solo look at one another, as Prawn playfully shoves at Luke's face. Princess Maki moves in between them and says, "Hey, I knew there was more to you than cowry shells."
Luke looks toward his X-Fin and becomes worried, saying, "Oh no!"
The fried Miso-D2 is lifted off the back of the X-Fin fighter and carried off under the worried eyes of Soy-3PO.
Soy-3PO exclaims, "Oh, my! Miso-D2! Can you hear me? Say something!" He asks the mechanic, "You can repair him, can't you?"

*The technician responds, "We'll get to work on him, right away."
Soy-3PO replies, "You must repair him! If any of my glass or soy will
help, I'll gladly donate them."*

Luke approaches and comforts Soy-3PO, "He'll be alright."

*Some time later, Luke Soywalker, Prawn Solo, and Unagibacca
enter the huge ruins of the main knife block temple. Hundreds of
groupers are lined up in rows. Towlettes are flying and at the far end
stands a vision in seaweed green, the beautiful young Seanator,
Princess Maki. Luke and the others solemnly waddle up the long aisle
and bow before Seanator Maki. From one side of the Knife Block Temple
rolls a shined-up and fully repaired Miso-D2. He makes his way up to the
group and stands next to an equally pristine Soy-3PO, who is rather
awestruck by the whole event. Unagibacca is confused. Udondonna and
several other dignitaries sit on the left of Princess Maki. Princess Maki is
dressed in a long green seaweed-colored nori and is staggeringly
beautiful. She rises and places a gold medallion around Prawn's neck.
He winks at her. She then repeats the ceremony with Luke, who is
moved by the event. They turn and face the assembled groupers, who all
bow before them. Unagibacca growls and Miso-D2 burps with happiness.*

The tall, dark man woke up groaning. The policeman helped him up
and put him in another chair near the handcuffed lady and asked
everyone to go to the other side of the restaurant. We all scurried over to
the other side. My father hugged my mother and then me. He knelt down
before me and said, "I saw what you did, Billy. Great job, son! You're a
hero!" Hiroshi-san then came over to me and said, "Billy-san... thank
you. You saved Moto Sushi. I will make a new roll in your honor. The
Moto Billy Roll and it will contain only the finest of ingredients... and
some kushi, of course."

I breathed deeply, looked at my dad, and then at Hiroshi-san and
said, "Hiroshi-san, I think I am ready to try that new roll."

GLOSSARY & NOTES

You won't find many fiction books with a section like this but I felt this one needed it. This book required a lot of research into sushi and the Star Wars universe. So, here is a collection of notes that perhaps, after reading, add value to the jokes, puns, and sushification of the Star Wars universe. I encourage you to look up the references for a deeper dive into the sushi world.

Starring Characters:

Admiral Madai - Admiral Motti made of a sea bream or whitefish

Baigai - Biggs as a water snail

Bifu Katsu - Beru Lars, Luke's aunt, made of fried beef

Breaded Leader - Red Leader as katsu breading

Captain Ama-ebi - Captain Antilles made of sweet shrimp, Captain of the Rebel Hammerhead Runner

Clampeople - Sandpeople made of clams

Dashi - Dutch the Gold Leader as soup and cooking stock

Engawa - Jawa made of the thin muscle of the dorsal fin of a halibut with green roe for eyes

Gillard the Clammander - Willard, the Commander of the Rebel forces on Massassi as fish gills

Gobo - Greedo as a burdock root creature

Goma Leader - Gold Leader Rebel star fighter made from unhulled sesame seeds

Grand Moff Tarako - Grand Moff Tarkin made of Alaskan pollack roe

Imperial Buricrats - Imperial Bureaucrats made of adult yellowfish

Imperial Gill Officer - Imperial Gantry Officer made of sea bass gill

Imperial Officer Bass - Imperial Officer Cass made from sea bass

Imperial Seigo Officers - Imperial Officers made of young sea bass

Jek Katsu-kins - Jek Porkins, the Red Six fighter pilot in Battle of Yavin made of fried pork katsu

Luke Soywalker - Luke Skywalker made of tofu or atsuage with red roe for eyes

Mantas - Banthas made of manta rays ridden by Clampeople

Miso-D2 - R2-D2 made of miso soup dish

O-Ton Katsu - Owen Lars, Luke's uncle, made of fried pork katsu

Obi-Wan Wasabi - Obi-Wan Kenobi made of wasabi with red roe for eyes

Odori-don – Dianoga, a live octopus creature in the Death Star garbage compactor

Ponda Bera - Ponda Baba, the alien that pushes Luke in the Cantina and loses his arm made of rainbow fish

Prawn Solo - Han Solo as a prawn with black roe for eyes

Princess Maki - Princess Leia made of California rolls with red roe for eyes

Rebel Groupers - Rebel Troopers made of grouper fish

Saketroopers - Stormtroopers made of sake bottles

Shucken Raiders - Tusken Raiders, another name for Clampeople

Soy-3PO - C-3PO made of a soy sauce bottle

Squid Vader - Darth Vader made of squid with orange roe for eyes

Tataki the Clammander - Commander Tagge made of finely sliced tuna

Tori - Tiree the Gold Two pilot made of chicken

Udondonna – Dodonna, the Rebel leader on Yavin moon Massassi made of thick, wide wheat noodles

Unagibacca - Chewbacca made of eel

Wookieels - Wookies made of eel with black roe for eyes

Warasa - Bartender named Wuher in the Mos Eisely Cantina made of yellowtail

Wasaba the Root - Jabba the Hutt as a wasabi root

Wedge the Lemontilles - Wedge Antilles as a lemon wedge

Zen Wasabi - Ben Kenobi is the same as Obi-Wan Wasabi

Groups:

The Surf – the Sith named after ocean currents

The Red-Eye Order – the Jedi Order having red roe for eyes

The Tempura - The Empire, but a little fried

Spacefish (Spaceships):

Death Starfish - the Death Star as a starfish

X-Fin Fighters - X-Wing Fighters as flying fish with the family name exocoetidae and it's roe is called tobikko

Gai Fighters - Tie Fighters made of semi-separated clams

Imperial Stargazers - Imperial Stardestroyers or Imperial Cruisers as a stargazer fish

Millennium Flounder - the Millennium Falcon as a flounder

Rebel Hammerhead Runners - Rebel Blockade Runners as hammerhead sharks

CraY-Fin Fighters - Y-Wing Fighters as crayfish swimming backwards

Other vehicles:

Duskyhopper - Skyhopper as a Dusky Grouper fish

Engawa Traysport – the Jawa Transport as a tray

Trayspeeder – Luke's Landspeeder as a small tray

Rainbow Runner - Rebel military armored speeder on Yavin as a Japanese scad

Plates (Planets) / Places:

Abaloneraan - Alderaan, a highly developed planet with ornate shell décor destroyed into saucers and dish fragments

Anchoviehead - Anchorhead mining settlement on Tatooine that smells like fish

Bamboo's Canyon - Beggar's Canyon on Tatooine lined with bamboo

Plates (Planets) / Places:

Chakin's Oceanport CannedTuna - Chalmun's Spaceport Cantina, the alternate name for Mos Eisely Cantina as a can of tuna fish

Corallia – Correllia, the planet of the Corellians made of coral

Funamori - Jundland wastelands on Tatooine in the form of a boat wrap

Massassea - Massassi, the 4th moon of Yavin and Rebel base as a seaweed jungle moon in the sea

Mos Icely - Mos Eisley spaceport on Tatooine made of mostly ice

Mos Icely CannedTuna - Mos Eisely Cantina on Tatooine as a can of tuna on ice

Mussel Run - Kessel Run, the space run made famous by the Millennium Falcon

Outer Reef Territories - Outer Rim Territories in the form of a reef

Pantooine - Dantooine, home of the Rebel base as disclosed by Princess Leia in the form of a frying pan

Tidetooine - Tatooine, a completely wet planet, with nearly no land, reminiscent of a tide pool instead of a desert planet

Yafin - Yavin, a bright red gas giant planet with a land mass that looks like a giant fin

Glossary of Items found in Sushi
Wars in sushified order:

aclamademy - academy
air sac - cabinet or storage
ambulacral groove - trench
ampulla - Death Star office
antenna - headset microphone
beancon - beacon
beaned - beamed
biological - magnetic
boiled - killed
brain - computer
burps - bleeps
Brown Rice – the Dark side
carbohydrates - faith
cartilage - debris
chalkboard - display
chopsaber - lightsaber
clambassador - ambassador
clammander - commander
clammands - commands
clammation - formation
clampedo – torpedo
clamvoy - convoy
conus-lar - consular
conuslink - comlink
cowry shells - money
crawfish - crewmen
dataseed - data chip
definsive - defensive
digestive gland - prison cell
echinodermic - metallic
electro-finoculars -electro-
    binoculars
escape egg - escape pod
es-cargo - cargo
esophagus - shaft
eye turret - gun turret
eye-scope - gun scope
fishhead eyes - windows
fin - hand
fincuffs - handcuffs
findles - handles

fineuvers - maneuvers
finipulate - manipulate
finmen - wingmen
finned - armed
first-bait - first-mate
fish - man
fish egg - baby
fishhead - cockpit
floundification - modification
fried - killed
fryghten - frighten
gai-ness - highness
galaxsea - galaxy
gari stick - gaderffii or gaff stick
gastroreactor - reactor
gill - spacefish engine
gunfin - gunport
gurgles - beeps
hermit crab - hermit
hisses - whirls
hydro - astro
hypersea - hyperspace
identifincation - identification
ikura blast - grenade blast
insushi - inhuman
interplatetary - interplanetary
intertidal zone - system
kitchen - maintenance room
knife block - ancient temple
kushiform - lifeform
lamp - sun
land solidifier - moisture vaporator
laserbean blaster – laser beam
    blaster
laserbeans - laser beams
madfish - madmen
membrane - monitor
menus - navigation charts
microwaves - turbine generators
minnow - boy
mouth - entry to shaft
napkin - table
nerves - controls
nervous system – sensor system

nori - cloak
oceanverse - universe, space
parasitic war - civil war
plate - planet or place
platter - star
plop - thunder
ponzu sauce torpedo - proton torpedo
pore - door
poreway - doorway
pyloric stomach - reactor
radial canal - cellblock hallway
reef - forest
The Rice - The Force
rice field - force field
ring canal - main hallway
riptide speed - light speed
roebots - robots
rollogram - hologram
rollship - worship
saucer plate - moon
saucerer - sorcerer
scancap - scanner box
seanate - senate
seanator - senator
secret plate - secret base
shelf - tower

shells – shields
soba noodle - rope, handcuffs
sonar - radar
soy sauce dish - moon
soyds - droids
soyl - oil
spacefish - spaceship
spicing - shocking
spoil - die
stack of plates - solar system
starch - religion
steam - smoke
stomach hold area - hold area
supertide - supernova
sushi - people
sushiforms - lifeforms
terrifried - terrified
tidemissions - transmissions
torture crab - torture robot
transfinner - transmitter
traysport - transport
tube foot - tower
White Rice - the Light side
womp gnats - womp rats

ABOUT THE AUTHOR

Keith Chapman is a writer. There... I said it.

65500442R00112

Made in the USA
San Bernardino, CA
07 January 2018